TWAYNE'S WORLD AUTHORS SERIES
A Survey of the World's Literature

Luis Davila, Indiana University

EDITOR

URUGUAY

Juan Carlos Onetti

TWAS 469

Juan Carlos Onetti

JUAN CARLOS ONETTI

By DJELAL KADIR
Purdue University

TWAYNE PUBLISHERS
A DIVISION OF G. K. HALL & CO., BOSTON

Library of Congress Cataloging in Publication Data

Kadir, Djelal.
    Juan Carlos Onetti.

    (Twayne's world authors series ; TWAS 469)
    Bibliography: p. 155 - 57.
    Includes index.
    1.   Onetti, Juan   Carlos, 1909 -   —Criticism   and   inter-
pretation.
PQ8519.059Z74   863   77-8228
ISBN 0-8057-6310-4

C
c

Contents

About the Author

Djelal Kadir is Associate Professor of Spanish and Comparative Literature at Purdue University. He received his undergraduate degree from Yale University (1969), where he studied Philosophy and Latin American literature. He did his doctoral work at the University of New Mexico (Ph.D., 1972).

Professor Kadir's work has concerned itself with comparative literary problems and inter-American literary relations. He is the editor of *Triple espera: novelas cortas de Hispanoamérica* (Harcourt Brace Jovanovich). His numerous articles have appeared in such journals as *Modern Fiction Studies, Revue de Littérature Comparée, Latin American Literary Review,* and *Studies in Twentieth Century Literature.* He served as Guest Editor of the Onetti issue of *Review* (Winter, 1975).

Preface

When time permits literary history to judge the twentieth century, a group of writers will emerge and be identified as the "possessed." The common obsession of this group will be described as a mania to express the ineffable, to move beyond solipsism, to expose in a language context what words can not tell, and to unmask words *as* words. Juan Carlos Onetti will undoubtedly figure in the ranks of this group. Literary criticism has, in fact, already delineated sufficient evidence to insure that in the judgment of those future literary historians Juan Carlos Onetti will be counted as an integral part of such a group. Although Onetti himself has never spoken about writing, his work bespeaks a fundamental concern with the art and act of writing. In all his works, and particularly in novels like *La vida breve (A Brief Life)*, *Para una tumba sin nombre (For A Nameless Tomb)*, and *Los adioses (The Good-byes)*, Onetti approaches the novel simultaneously on practical and theoretical planes. As such, Onetti is very much within the tradition of the self-reflective novel. His work contains a commentary on the method of its own creation.

The primary focus of this study is on Onetti as novelist. There is an integral cohesion within the entirety of the Uruguayan writer's work which makes it possible to speak about the totality of his literary cosmos when focusing on any of its parts. Onetti is above all a novelist. His short stories are in one way or another fragments of a greater whole which is more extensively delineated in the novels. I shall therefore try to concentrate on the more massive elaborations of this totality, and on the means and methods of its conception.

Once a writer has a message, a vision he wishes to impart, writing a novel boils down to a series of decisions. Although the writer is the central figure of this decision making, he himself is subject to forces and influences which affect his choices. In this process, a writer, like a sorcerer or witchdoctor (as every novelist must be considered to be, because of his intent to evoke or create a contiguous cosmos to the universe), utilizes certain potions, tricks, and invocations in order to achieve what Sartre has called a "fictional system."[1] The cosmos which emerges in the final analysis is intrinsically tied to every minute gesture and decision of the writer. Thus, the totality we call the "fictional system" of an individual author is in some way unique. To attempt a comprehension of that uniqueness is to reach both for an understanding of the author and of his individual system of literature. Joseph Conrad's admission with respect to this problem, I think, demonstrates the point I am trying to make. Conrad tells us that: "In truth every novelist must begin by creating for himself a world, great or little, in which he can honestly believe. This world can not be made otherwise than in his own image: it is fated to remain individual and a little mysterious, and yet it must resemble something already familiar to the experience, the thoughts and the sensations of his readers."[2]

A novelist's fictional system is comprised of the elements and ingredients which make up fiction and the novelist's peculiar use and manner of treatment of them. These elements are and traditionally have been people or characters, a time and a place in which they are situated and operate, a plot which evolves from their interaction, a point of view which is our peephole to all that is occurring, and finally, a style with which all of these elements are tinged and presented.

In the rise of the contemporary Latin American novel, Juan Carlos Onetti is a key figure, if not *the* key figure as the Peruvian novelist Mario Vargas Llosa claims. With Onetti, reality and a vision of the world which comprise fiction are subjected to a consciously derived system of aesthetics for the first time in Latin America. The scope of this study is in part the nature of that aesthetics. It attempts to some extent to see Onetti in the light of the twentieth-century novel and novelistic technique. I will endeavor to present this Uruguayan novelist in the broader context of our century's literary problems. His preoccupations transcend national boundaries. In presenting the first book-length study in English on this significant writer, I will attempt in my consideration of his work to view the author in a literary context of works familiar to the reader of English.

The first chapter attempts a general overview by examining the development of Onetti's unique style and its function within the author's world. While it concentrates on the epistemology of the author's language and its relationship to the author's own life, the second chapter focuses on the basis which underlies the writer's human types. The discussion then centers on his technique and philosophy of characterization.

In the third chapter the focus is on Onetti's treatment of the temporal and spatial dimensions. His technique here is inevitably tied to his vision of time and space vis-à-vis the human condition and man's capacity to create and live within the world of myth.

The manner of narration and the author's relationship to his story and to the reader occupy the fourth chapter. The seemingly mechanical, cinematographic modes of recounting and observation, the all-pervasive camera eye, the confessional tone of the narrator-protagonists, as well as the omniscient voice of the author are discussed in this chapter.

The fifth chapter concerns itself with Onetti's construction of plot and the close relationship between his idea of the art of fiction and its execution. The author's defiance of chronology once again emerges. We also witness anew his obsession with myth and the capacity of his fictional worlds to multiply into independent units. Thus we observe subplots emerging as complete plots in themselves.

The sixth chapter attempts to tie the two ends, starting point and the conclusion to date, by examining Onetti's publications and his latest novel. I intend to show how the two points converge in an ironic act of cosmic self-betrayal.

In the conclusion, there is an attempt to view Onetti and his aesthetics, especially the aesthetics of the mythical, in the light of more recent fiction and the younger novelists. In short, the conclusion tries to relate Onetti to the vanguard of the genre within the context of modern literature.

I have translated the passages cited from Onetti's work. To date only *El astillero (The Shipyard)* and *La vida breve (A Brief Life)* have appeared in English. For consistency's sake, however, I have taken the responsibility of translating quoted passages from these novels as well.

DJELAL KADIR

Purdue University

Chronology

1909   July 1, Juan Carlos Onetti born in Montevideo.

1930   Travels to Buenos Aires for the first time.

1932   Writes the first version of *El pozo (The Pit)*. The original manuscript is lost.

1933   Publishes first short story, "Avenida de Mayo—Diagonal—Avenida de Mayo" ("May Avenue—Diagonal—May Avenue") in *La Prensa* of Buenos Aires.

1939   Named chief editor of the newly founded weekly *Marcha*. December, publishes *El pozo (The Pit)*, a reconstructed version of his first novel.

1940   Publishes "Convalecencia" ("Convalescence") in *Marcha* under the pseudonym of H. C. Ramos. His novel *Tiempo de abrazar (Time to Embrace)* comes in second to the Peruvian Ciro Alegría's *El mundo es ancho y ajeno (Broad and Alien Is the World)* in a contest sponsored by Rinehart and Farrar of New York.

1941   Moves back to Buenos Aires, working for Reuter's news agency, and, later, is editor of various periodicals. Remains in Buenos Aires until 1954. The novel *Tierra de nadie (No Man's Land)* is published by Losada and is awarded the second prize in the contest sponsored by the publisher.

1943   Publishes *Para esta noche (For This Night)*. Fragments of *Tiempo de abrazar ("Time to Embrace")* appear in *Marcha*.

1950   *La vida breve (A Brief Life)*.

1951   *Un sueño realizado y otros cuentos (A Dream Come True and Other Stories)*.

1953   Publishes the short novel *Los adioses (The Good-byes)* and "El álbum" ("The Album"), short story, in *Sur*.

1954   In Montevideo, works for a publicity firm and later for the periodical *Acción*.

1957   Named director of municipal libraries in Montevideo and to the board of directors of the Comedia Nacional.

1959   *Una tumba sin nombre (A Nameless Tomb)*.

1960   *La cara de la desgracia (The Face of Misfortune)*.

1961   *El astillero (The Shipyard)* is selected by the jury of a literary contest sponsored by Compañia General Fabril Editora and published by the company.

1962   Awarded the *Premio Nacional de Literatura,* Uruguay's national literary prize, for work published in 1959 - 1960.

1963   *El astillero (The Shipyard)* is awarded "The William Faulkner Foundation Certificate of Merit." *Tan triste como ella (As Sad as She),* novella, is published.

1964   *Juntacadáveres (The Corpse Collector).*

1967   *Juntacadáveres* is runner-up in the prestigious Romulo Gallegos Prize which selects the best novel written in Spanish every five years.

1970   *Obras completas (Complete Works).*

1973   *La muerte y la niña (Death and the Girl).*

1974   Publishes *Tiempo de abrazar (Time to Embrace)* upon recovery of greater part of the manuscript lost since 1940. Edition also includes "Los niños en el bosque" ("The Children in the Woods") a fragment written in 1936 which most likely was to have been a novel, as well as all short stories written between 1933 and 1955 but were never collected into a volume or the *Complete Works.* January, imprisoned by military authorities over the awarding of a literary prize to a story deemed inappropriate by the authorities (Onetti was a judge in the contest). May, released from prison.

1975   *El astillero (The Shipyard)* awarded Italy's prize for best foreign work translated into Italian that year. Refused leave to attend award ceremony. Resigns directorship of municipal libraries and travels to Europe where he stays in Madrid.

1976   *Requiem por Faulkner y otros escritos (Requiem for Faulkner and Other Writings).* Remains in Madrid.

CHAPTER 1

Origin and Circumstances: The Poetics of the Pouting Lip and Suspended Cigarette

I *The Man*

A NY study which focuses simultaneously on the biography and literary achievement of Juan Carlos Onetti will inevitably favor the latter. The literary work of the author overshadows the life of the man. While this inevitability might pose problems for biographers and disappointment for readers in pursuit of biographical curiosities, the serious reader of Onetti may find a certain delight in this predicament.

Some writers acquire an aura which transforms them into mythical figures matched only by the most notorious characters of their work, a parity which in the mind of the casual reader makes author and heroes indistinguishable. Certain writers collaborate in their transformation by taking an active role in this process; others collaborate through indifference and passive acquiescence. Juan Carlos Onetti belongs to the latter category. The intensity of his indifference and of his sardonic acquiescence, coupled with the avid enthusiasm of his followers, has all but obliterated biographical traces of the man, converting his life into a shadow of the world and lives he has authored. Onetti would not have it any other way. He has always operated on the principle that facts are really empty, mere possibilities that may or may not have any truth to them. Like the world of his protagonists, whose only meaningful undertaking consists of imagining other hypothetical lives, whether for themselves or for the imaginary figures of their fantasies, Onetti's sullen, resigned indifference would appear to indicate two alternatives for the critical reader: (1) read the literary work of the author as the inner, spiritual itinerary of the man; or (2) construct a series of hypotheses from a number of facts about a man who forewarns us repeatedly through his work that there is a clear distinction between fact and truth. The present study has opted principally for the first of these possibilities. The second alternative, however, while it cannot be ignored, if followed wholeheartedly, would convert the "biographer" into a mirror image of the fantasy-ridden author and his characters. Onetti remains the best author of his own novels. Thus I will only attempt to reconstruct briefly whatever "facts" may possibly salvage some element of verity out of the remains of a reality disintegrated into literature.

Juan Carlos Onetti was born on July 1, 1909, in Montevideo. He is the second of three children. His father, Carlos Onetti, was a customs official. His mother, Honoria Borges de Onetti, was the descendant of Brazilian landowners from Rio Grande do Sul. It was a happy family, according to Onetti, even though they had to move frequently within Montevideo. As a child, Juan Carlos was wont to tell tales about other people ("lies," according to him). He was a poor student, particularly in geography and drawing, and eventually abandoned school. He worked at a number of odd jobs, including those of porter, waiter, ticket taker, and wheat sifter.

In 1930 Onetti married his cousin, María Amalia Onetti, and left for Buenos Aires, the first of many trips to the Argentine capital where he lived for varied durations each time. His first job in Buenos Aires was that of selling adding machines. In 1932 Onetti wrote the first version of *El pozo (The Pit)* which, like many subsequent manuscripts of his, was misplaced and lost. At the same time he was working on another novel, *Tiempo de abrazar (Time to Embrace)* which came to the attention of Roberto Arlt, the Argentine writer who would prove a key influence in Onetti's development as novelist. In 1934 Onetti returned to Montevideo after the breaking up of his first marriage. In Montevideo he married for the second time. His new bride was María Julia Onetti, the sister of his first wife.

In the second half of the 1930s Onetti acquired a very small but avid following. Montevideo's Café Metro became a focal point of intellectual gatherings. Onetti's contacts with the young intellectuals here would prove very influential in his subsequent portrayal of the lost generation, especially in works like *Tierra de nadie (No Man's Land)*.

In 1939 Onetti was active in founding and running the influential weekly *Marcha*. He was made editor in chief of this important publication which ran until 1974. In 1941 Onetti was employed by Reuters, the British news service, and moved back to Buenos Aires where he was made bureau chief. At the same time he was named editor in chief of the Argentine magazine *Vea y Lea* and director of a publicity magazine, *Impetu*.

In 1945 Onetti married for the third time and in 1951 his wife, Elizabeth María Pekelhering, gave birth to their daughter Isabel María (Litti). Onetti remained in Buenos Aires until 1954 when he returned to Montevideo and embarked on his fourth marriage to Dorotea (Dolly) Muhr. He began working for the periodical *Acción* the following year and in 1956 he traveled for the first time out of the twin cities of the River Plate. He went to Bolivia. In 1957 he was appointed director of municipal libraries of Montevideo, a position he held until 1975.

The 1960s, with the so called "boom" of the Latin American novel, brought Onetti long-deserved recognition: his works were reissued in multiple printings; he was awarded Uruguay's Premio Nacional de Literature, the national literary prize, in 1962; and, in 1966, he was invited to attend the meeting of the P.E.N. Club in New York, Onetti's first trip to the United States. In 1968 *El astillero (The Shipyard)*, his first major work to be translated into English, appeared in New York. In 1973 Onetti traveled to Spain at the invitation of the Instituto de Cultura Hispánica where he delivered a series of lectures.

Eventual success has not proved easy, however. In 1974, by now a very visible figure in Uruguay's cultural life, Onetti fell prey to the social upheaval of that unfortunate country. His imprisonment by the military authorities because a literary prize was awarded to a work deemed improper by the dictatorship (Onetti was among the judges making the award) aggravated his already debilitated physical condition. Owing to the outcry from the international community of intellectuals and to his poor health, Onetti was finally released. In 1975 he was at last forced to resign his post as director of municipal libraries and he subsequently abandoned Uruguay for Europe.

Presently, Onetti lives in a Madrid apartment with his wife and is working on a long novel.

II   *The Writer*

The 1930s, when Juan Carlos Onetti's fiction begins to appear, represents a breach in the literary history of Spanish America. This same decade is also a culmination of certain historical factors which alter the course of Spanish American society: the late nineteenth- and early twentieth-century influx of European immigrants to the already disproportionately large cities of Buenos Aires and Montevideo; the advent of World War I; and the economic collapse of the early thirties. The conditions created by these events have an indelible effect on the intellectual consciousness of Spanish America. The countries most affected, however, are those which have the closest ties to Europe. Argentina and Uruguay, as a consequence of the European configuration of their populace, recently replenished by the immigration waves, had at that time and for some time to come a direct cultural lifeline to European centers. The breakdown of the old order, the dissipation of traditional values, the sundering of an integrated self-identity of societies in the Western world following World War I were not exclusively European events. Nor was the rise of "the lost generation" an occurrence unique to the United States. The youth of those twin cities of Buenos Aires and Montevideo underwent a similar process of disillusionment and disorientation.

The two cosmopolitan centers of Buenos Aires and Montevideo had always had their backs turned to the rest of the country. Although they face the murky waters of the River Plate, by now they had convinced themselves that they faced the Atlantic and Europe. In the face of the European and North American upheaval, the poetic naturalism of *gauchos* and the *pampas* seemed inert and of another time. The focus of literature turned away from nature. Its primary concern as of this decade would not be man's struggle for survival in the face of an inclement nature and its incomprehensible forces. The new generation of writers was forced to confront inner nature, the fundamental identity of man in the face of odds precipitated by his own actions and the interrogatives engendered by his own consciousness. The dialectic now shifts from man against nature to man vis-à-vis the human condition. Accordingly, the scenario of literature shifts from the country to the amorphous urban sprawl, to the displaced individual struggling to define his own circumstance within the impersonal and alienating melee of urbanity. The ineluctable forces of subjectivism and individuation produce a new breed of man. They engender a self-conscious, reflective individual who inevitably strives to objectify his own existence, abetting the forces of alienation and estrangement by the inexplicable need to transform himself into the subject of his own understanding. The beneficiary of this inevitable process is literature, particularly the novelistic genre which, as a rule, has found its most fertile ground in the estrangement characteristic of large urban centers.

Out of the silent dialogue with the self, as with the desperate gesticulations of two mutes, there comes a genuine literature, grounded in the very essence of the human condition. The result is a literature inherently born of a compelling necessity. As the origins of this literature are drab, so are its heroics and its heroes. A new species of protagonists is born to reflect the new species of writer. Authors cast their heroes in their own image, or at least in the image of their imagined self: solitary, estranged, morally indifferent, confined to the silence of a nagging consciousness, suspicious and suspecting, withdrawn, and cynical only because what they are capable of idealizing and what actuality offers are separated by an unbreachable abyss. They retire to the confines of rented rooms or wander stooped-over through anonymous city streets like the underground men of nineteenth-century Russia. They are men of a peculiar brand of unyielding faith, a faith which rather than being misdirected remains stagnant and undirected. It serves to widen the gap between expectations and reality, and to plunge the individual into the maelstrom of reflections and labyrinthine constructs that result in a literature through which we partake of the absurdity of this human condition.

Juan Carlos Onetti was nourished and formed by these circumstances. His first short story, "Avenida de Mayo—Diagonal—Avenida de Mayo," appeared in 1933 and won a literary prize sponsored by *La Prensa* of Buenos Aires. While Onetti is generally recognized by critics and accepted by younger novelists as one of the founders of this new literature, he was preceded by an ingenious writer who initiated the novel of the city: *his* career, like his life, was short lived. Before dying at the age of forty-two, however, he was able to leave for posterity and literary history three novels, two collections of short stories, eight dramatic works, and some two thousand articles. I am referring to Roberto Arlt, that first chronicler of Buenos Aires who was doing for the River Plate city what Joyce was engaged in doing for Dublin at the same time, and what Dos Passos would later do for Manhattan and Döblin for Berlin.

In the year of the publication of his first short story Juan Carlos Onetti finished writing *Tiempo de abrazar (Time to Embrace)* one of his first novels, which was read by Roberto Arlt in 1934. Arlt recommended its publication but the work was never published. In the following two years, two more stories by Onetti appeared: "El obstáculo" in 1935 and "El posible Baldi" in 1936. The tenor of these short pieces and of Onetti's first published novel, *El pozo (The Pit)*, (1939), have come to be regarded as the paradigms of the author's subsequent literary cosmos. From the very beginning the alienated, existentially tortured human type represents the Onettian hero.

Between the year of this first novel and 1944, a span of about five years, Onetti plunges himself into feverish activity. He publishes a second novel, *Tierra de nadie (No Man's Land)* in 1941 and a third in 1943, *Para esta noche (For this Night)*. In 1941 the ill-fated *Tiempo de abrazar* disappears after losing a literary prize to an already forgotten author and work. It is not until 1974 that a greater part of this manuscript is finally recovered and published.

The year 1939 begins another era in Uruguayan letters with the founding of the weekly *Marcha,* which appeared continuously until 1974. After serving as chief editor of that journal for its first two years, Onetti moves to Buenos Aires where he remains until 1954. With this move, Onetti becomes the chronicler of the twin River Plate cities. He is later (in 1950 and with the appearance of his fourth novel, *La vida breve)* to synthesize the two urban centers and invent his own cosmogony, the mythical Santa María, whose annals will be divulged by his subsequent works.

The end of the third decade and beginning of the fourth is a key period in the cultural history of Argentina and Uruguay as well as in the development of Onetti's work. By 1939 Franco has overpowered Spain, and the voice of Ortega y Gasset and of the influential *Revista de Occidente,* published under his aegis, are silenced. García Lorca is murdered, Unamuno dies, and so does Antonio Machado. Hitler is in Paris by 1940. Writers like Sartre and André Gide are either in prison camps or in forced exile. The greatest fears of those young intellectuals who suffered the shock of disillusionment between the end of the World War I and beginning of the second are now realities to be born and dealt with. It is under these historical realities that Onetti's work begins to take form. His world vision is inextricably tied to the embattled events of these times. Onetti, however, never gives himself up to causes. His commitment is always to the more fundamental struggle of man in the face of his own absurdity. In this respect Geoffrey Hartman's affirmation about Northrop Frye is also appropriate for Juan Carlos Onetti: "a gnostic, who prefers myth to the scandal of a historical revelation."[1]

The second decade of the author's publishing career, the 1950s, manifests more clearly the trajectory of Onetti's maturation as a master of the craft of fiction. A number of possible technical tendencies implicit in his first three published novels, now become more delineated. His peculiarities are brought into sharper focus beginning with *La vida breve* which initiates the decade. There is a cumulative development in the writer's career. As we examine some of the particular works more closely in the following chapters of this study, I believe this accretion will become more evident. This period is comprised of one novel, already mentioned, two novellas (*Los adioses*, 1954; *Una tumba sin nombre* 1959), a collection of short stories, *Un sueño realizado y otros cuentos* (*A Dream Come True and Other Stories*, 1951), and five short pieces which will later prove to be fragments of two novels that appear in the early 1960s and are widely accepted as the apotheosis of Onetti's saga of the mythical Santa María, *El astillero* (1961) and *Juntacadáveres* (1964).

The 1950s is a highly poetic period for Onetti. He confronts the problems of language and of the elusiveness of meaning in reality. Technically this leads him to a perspectivism of narration which exposes the multiplicity of meanings and the total absence of absolutes in the realm of man's experiences. This dispersion of meanings and the multiplicity of perspectives had formed an integral part of previous novels like *El pozo* and *Tierra de nadie*. In the first we witness the impossibility of capturing a lasting reality; in *Tierra de nadie*, as we shall see in a subsequent chapter, we find a multiple series of human destinies and their disparate loci which pile up to form a totality. Thus parallelism in isolation becomes consolidated in subsequent works into a poetic perspectivism that hints at many simultaneous realities within the same set of human circumstances.

Onetti is an obsessed mythopoeist, a manufacturer of myths. His, however, are myths of a very special kind. They are language constructs in which more than one generation of disoriented and self-conscious youth of Latin American cities will be able to find their literary counterpart. The myth of the imagined Santa María, a verbal creation of one of Onetti's mythomaniac protagonists (Brausen of *La vida breve*), is a contiguous reality to the realities of cosmopolitan Buenos Aires and Montevideo. It is a linguistic reality however, a world conceived and delineated through a very special kind of language which corresponds to a special mode of being. I should now like to turn more specifically to these two simultaneous states of language and existence in Onetti and to the unique style through which they manifest themselves in the Uruguayan author's life and work.

A recent term students of literature have adapted from linguistics is "idiolect," defined as "the peculiar use of language by a particular speaker."[2] A writer's peculiar idiolect speaks not only for him, but it also speaks to us of him, of his uniqueness as a novelist and of his personal and characteristic vision of the reality which is the subject of this idiolect. Like every novelist, Juan Carlos Onetti has established his own idiolect and with it stylistic peculiarities which manifest themselves uniformly in the incongruous poetic syntax of his work.

Let it suffice for me to say that since literature is a product of language, the idiolect of an author has implicit in it the "style" of that author. Style is not merely what is seen in the end product of a writer's work. It also implies something about the nature of the writer and his literary perspective on the world. A mode of expression implies a mode of perception on the part of a novelist. This being the case, it is difficult to speak of a man's style without speaking of the man, the human essence which gives rise to that style. It becomes even more imperative when we take into consideration the emotional tone, the "temper of mind"[3] which gives the idiolect a more personal and uniquely human quality emanating from those particular gestalts we call feelings.

Style, therefore, is constituted primarily of two elements: an idiolect or language, and an emotional tone. With respect to the first, Richard Ohmann[4] quite convincingly demonstrates that the formation of a writer's idiolect is through an *epistemic choice*. That is to say, there is a peculiar way of "knowing" the world in the language that a particular writer "chooses" to utilize. An author, through language, is capable of swaying the reader to experience the universe in definite ways to the exclusion of others. Certain linguistic patterns which he habitually uses become in themselves epistemologies with specific meaning. Thus, the habits that the writer develops in sorting and portraying the phenomena of the world are just as meaningful as the ideas or words which the writer overtly expresses. In the case of Juan Carlos Onetti these peculiarities are quite emphatic and clearly manifest both in his works and in his everyday life.

The factors determining these modes of understanding and relating the world are innumerable and not easily identifiable. However, some factors that play a role in the stylistic choice of the writer can objectively be viewed and discussed. The choice of subject matter, the themes, the human types he wishes to portray can and do determine stylistic decisions.

Once the epistemic choice of language is made there remains the manner of its presentation. The emotional tone, as Susanne Langer argues,[5] takes on its value from the way in which an idea or a statement is presented. With reference to the less definable and not so overt determinants of style, Mr. Ohmann tells us that a style articulates itself, even when a writer does not consciously attempt to give it a particular mode or manner of expression: "For the limits of speakable thought are not the boundaries of experience, or even of rational experience, and thoughts not included in the totality of verifiable propositions [in speakable or spoken terms] are nonetheless an integral part of style, as of knowledge."[6]

The realm of these "unverifiable propositions" I would call feelings or emotions which underlie the surface of the spoken and speakable thoughts. That is not to say, and this is the point to be made, that these subverifiable or subsurface propositions do not articulate themselves. They do, indeed. I would say this holds most true in the genre of the novel where the artist is involved in recreating life or creating a verisimilar, contiguous reality to it. The novel contains the human imprint in a more overt manner, that is, more human situations of everyday life, than any other art form. This is what Joseph Conrad means when he says that in the artistic creation of a novelist his world "must resemble something already familiar to the experience, the thoughts and the sensations of his readers."

This organic relationship of thought, language, and feeling is imperative if an author is to be convincing. Thus the statement by Richard Ohmann: "Complete honesty demands that the writer not only state his ideas accurately, but also take an emotional stance."[7]

Juan Carlos Onetti establishes the epistemic choices of his style with his first novel. The "temper of mind" or emotional tonality of his work is also founded at this time. What stylistic peculiarities are manifest in *El pozo* become stylistic patterns which readily identify Onetti's subsequent literary production.

El pozo is the futile story of a solitary protagonist, Eladio Linacero, who is at the threshold of integrating the disparate

elements of his life: his memories, his dreams, his identity as an
asocial, indifferent human being. Shut off in the stifling air of his
garret on the eve of his fortieth birthday, he is gripped by the
realization of an acute awareness of himself, of his pungent body
and unshaven face as well as of his fantasies of distant, ephemeral
places and the memories of his youth which he considers idiotic.
With self-mocking irony he sits down to consolidate the fragments
of an alienated self, adrift on the borders of humanity, into an
autobiography. He confesses that he does not know how to write,
but that does not really matter to him since he is writing about
himself. His admission is genuine. It gives a quality of sincerity to
his confessions. Linacero is most convincing when it comes to
relating the impossibility of his task, his own inability to capture the
cumulative result of the last forty years. What he pursues is "the
story of a soul, all by itself, without any of the events it had to be involved in whether it wanted to or not." Linacero's undertaking
serves only to remove him further from the world, from a social context of "events." In his acute awareness of his existence and of the
objective world around him, he opens the gap separating him from
the rest of humanity, isolating himself even further. By the end of
his attempt to capture the "story of a soul," Linacero comes to the
realization that while he was engaged in his task, time has added
yet another night to his existence as an outsider. He ends by returning once again to stretch out in his bed and look at the wall, the
posture from which he had tired and gotten up at the beginning of
the novel to compose the confessions he recorded.

Beginning with this work, Onetti speaks to the reader through a
narrator-confessor, in the first person. The narration of this and subsequent confessor-characters have a simultaneity in time which
makes them overlap the narration of the author and the narrative
present confronting the reader. There seems to be a fusion of
epistemologies. The idiolect is personal and at an intimate plane of
self-confession.

In this respect the first sentence of *El pozo* is revealing: "I was
just walking back and forth through the room, and it suddenly occurred to me that I was seeing it for the first time" ("Hace un rato
me estaba paseando por el cuarto y se me occurrió de golpe que lo
veía por primera vez").[8] Obviously this is not what one would identify as particularly literary language. It is the language of everyday
life. The tone of the narrative voice speaks with familiarity, as we
would speak or as Eladio Linacero, the narrator-protagonist, would

speak to an acquaintance if not to a friend. Thus, the author establishes a definite frame of mind in the very first sentence. The
reader has no other adjustments to make to the novelist's language
or tonality hereafter. Furthermore, there is a complete temper of
honesty in this first sentence. It is a kind of honesty that makes the
reader a participant in the work from the beginning. Linacero
speaks in the imperfect past tense to tell us what he was just doing:
"Just a while ago . . ." ("Hace un rato . . ."). Where does this
put him in relation to the writer? Precisely where in "actuality" the
moment in time and place finds them. Linacero is no longer walking about his room, but he tells us he just was, so we automatically
switch our psychological time to an actual present in which
Linacero is writing or telling: "Just a while ago I was walking"
("Hace un rato estaba paseando . . .") and we as readers are there
to witness that moment in time. What about Onetti, the author? He
has now, as a result of this first sentence, established a frequency on
which he and his reader can mutually operate on in simultaneity.
The reader is now in his confidence, and he in the reader's. There
are no "outsiders" in the affair; everyone is an "accomplice";
everyone partakes of this alienation.

Epistemologically, this first sentence of Onetti's novel is posi-
tively a most destructive sentence. It obliterates all existence and
epistemologies prior to this very moment. As such, the field of
meaning now remains blank; it is wide open, the universe is a white
canvas on which Eladio Linacero may commence to articulate and
found a novel significance and meaning within the circumstances in
which he finds himself. The last half of the sentence following the
conjunction "and" ("y") ". . . it suddenly occurred to me that I
was seeing it for the first time" (". . . se me ocurrió de golpe que
lo veía por primera vez") holds an infinite promise of things to come,
in terms of Eladio Linacero's life, in terms of the novel in which
he appears, and in terms of his creator's literary career, of which
Linacero is the archetypal hero. The room in which Linacero is
physically present, the cosmos of which it is a microcosm, now
awaits its definition—a definition of what this new way, as seen for
the first time, contains. Without departing from the new vision of
the cosmos, Linacero continues: "There are two cots, wobbly chairs
without a seat, months-old newspapers discolored by the sun, nailed
to the window where glass should be." Disappointing? Not quite.
Fatal, futile, indifferent would be more apt. There emerges from
this very beginning a unique style. One can see the presence of a

personal idiolect, an unnerving emotional tone, and an epistemological system, *sui generis*, with a "novel" vision of the world. This exasperating tone will remain constant in Onetti's work.

In 1966, twenty-seven years after *El pozo*, Onetti's attitude toward reality remains constant, as his words to María Esther Gilio proclaim through this fragment of the following interview. The concurrence between Onetti's proclamation and the vision of reality posited by the protagonist of his first novel is anything but cryptic:

Gilio: As far as your own relationship with the world. . . .
Onetti: You say that I am not immersed in it; that I refuse to accept it.
Gilio: Yes, and I also say that in order to construct your literature you do not look to the outside but to the world that you have in your entrails. You ignore history.
Onetti: The world that I have in my entrails. . . . The phrase is novel and it is forceful. But, that world that I have in my entrails, my dear lady, is a consequence of what you call the outside world. A world in which I find myself and accept. I reserve the right to criticize it and I do it in that indirect and skeptical style of mine with which you are familiar.
Gilio: Your literary world is also distorted. Doesn't so much distortion seem suspicious to you? Do you really think that you accept the outside world?
Onetti: This makes me think of the definition of a famous French painter: "The artist must act toward reality in the same way that a lover acts toward a woman: he makes love to her but does not respect her." Shall we change the subject?[9]

These are the words and vision of the man who stares blankly behind his heavy-rimmed glasses, pouts like a distorted Olmec face, and invariably dangles a cigarette from his lower lip. Perhaps his compatriot Carlos Maggi has painted the most accurate picture of him in Onetti's own style:

He is there; he pants. A grave sound, yellow and wide like the horn of a ship in fog is heard; a sick whale—O'Neill would say—grumbling in the pit below; a dilapidated, grand crustacean, a dejected horse with heavy eyes, intimidated; something tender collapsed on the skylight of a dirty apartment house, shipwrecked under the sad dust that drizzles on the cities. . . . He eats his food cold, smokes thoroughly, drinks red wine in abundance without looking for anyone, as if crying in reverse, inward, for what escapes and is lost while the smoke dissolves within the four walls of his pit of air. . . . Passionately dispassionate, believes that he does not believe in anything and only has faith in the lack of faith. There are very few things that matter to him (perhaps pure purity with the guarantee of its impossibility) and nonetheless he keeps a vigil for all things. He halts the night on a school notebook, composes, provokes the life within his life.[10]

No other description of Onetti could be more apt. It is interesting to note in these passages that Onetti inspires a characterization of himself with all the lineaments of his characters and their world. Since such characterization is so befitting and accurate, it does, indeed, indicate something about Onetti vis-à-vis his heroes, antiheroes, and fictitious world.

Luis Harss in *Into the Mainstream* depicts Juan Carlos Onetti as a type of Gogolian Akaky Akakievich who roves the streets of Petersburg wrapped in the black overcoat. Onetti himself frequently depicts his characters in a similar fashion: "In the slow drizzle, trudging down the street in a bulky coat, stooped under the weight of the city is a sleepwalker on a sleepless night. Like the city, he looks tired and middle-aged. He is tall, gaunt, with splotches of white in his gray hair, insomniac eyes straining behind horn-rimmed glasses, painfully grimacing lips, a high professorial forehead, and the slouch of an aging clerk."[11]

Juan Carlos Onetti has a tremendous affinity with the men and women that populate his imaginary cosmos just as they do to each other. As a matter of fact, the "aging clerk" by the name of Onetti makes his appearance in *La vida breve* (1950). One of the characters, Juan María Brausen, tells us that he shares an office with a disinterested man named Onetti. The author himself on the jacket of *Tierra de nadie* (1941), his second novel, writes: "In the most important country of South America, out of the American youth rises a human type of moral indifference, a type of man without faith or interest in his destiny. Let no one reproach this novelist for having faced the portrayal of that human type with the same spirit of indifference."

There is a very strong empathy here which engenders a concurrence between Onetti's life and the type of existence he infuses into the characters of his fiction. All of this seems to indicate that there is a definite uniformity of style arising from a unique view and conception of the world and of reality in both the life and work of Onetti. The prevalence of this uniformity will become more apparent as we study Onetti's work more closely. The consistency holds not only as regards his life, person, and characters. It also

permeates the author's fictional system itself and results in a significant stylistic homogeneity. On this point the influence of Henry
James, a writer which has always fascinated Onetti, becomes overtly
manifest. James summed up his theory of fiction in one paragraph:
"I cannot imagine composition existing in a series of blocks, nor
conceive, in any novel worth discussing at all, of a passage of
description that is not in its intention narrative, a passage of
dialogue that is not in its intention descriptive, a touch of truth of
any sort that does not partake of the nature of incident. . . . A
novel is a living thing, all one and continuous, . . . in each of the
parts there is something of each of the other parts."[12]

The structural homogeneity which James prescribes for himself is
Juan Carlos Onetti's strongest characteristic, as one can see from the
little variation engendered in the criticism of his work. The unity of
which James speaks and to which Onetti adheres is the traditional
assimilation of the component genres of the novel in their appropriate balance: the essayistic material, that James calls "a touch
of the truth," the dramatic material or dialogue, and the narrative
or "incident," all three functioning in some measure to produce a
unity, that is to say, an organism embued with life. Juan Carlos
Onetti has achieved this uniformity both internally in the struc-
turing of his novels and externally in his personal existence as it
relates to his creation and inasmuch as his work is a reflection of his
essence as man.

Having spoken of Onetti himself in terms of his life and work, I
would like to glance briefly at the way this style functions within his
fictional system and then try to arrive at some tentative conclusion
as to what a uniform style implies. Why does the author, very much
in the nineteenth-century tradition of Melville and James, adhere
stylistically to his first work and both to the epistemologies and
themes that were announced in it?

The uniformity of style founded by Onetti in his first novel is
structurally easily explainable. There is only one character, the
protagonist Eladio Linacero, who is also the narrator. The narrative
is in both past and present tense, but even when other characters
are mentioned or speak from the past, they are filtered through the
psyche and consciousness of the protagonist. The tone is the same
throughout, since the action takes place only at two levels: in the
actual time and place of Linacero's room, and in his fantasy or
dream world. In both cases the pattern of speech is identical. In this
sense the work is a closed world with definite elements to the exclu-

sion of others. Thus the style is entirely dependent upon one level of consciousness, that of Eladio Linacero and his sensations; the singularity of style in the work does not vary and is to be expected. Although it becomes more difficult to maintain this type of unity in a novel where there is more than one narrative plane, more than one perspective, and various levels of actual dramatic and open-ended essayistic material, Onetti nonetheless succeeds in sustaining this unity in such elaborate works as *Tierra de nadie, Para una tumba sin nombre*, and *Juntacadáveres*. In this respect, Onetti is a master of the novel, capable of handling more complex and compounded patterns with the same ease as the single modality that operates in his first work.

The author's penultimate novel from the saga of his mythical Santa María, *Juntacadáveres* (1964), is multifaceted in its narrative perspective. Yet, the unity, the uniformity of style to which I refer, is no less notable than in *El pozo*.

Juntacadáveres is narrated from two distinct points of view: that of the author-narrator who commences the work and makes his most Gide-like omniscience apparent in Chapter 20, and that of Jorge Malabia who becomes the Eladio Linacero figure of this work. His narrative is in the first person; the level of speech is at the same personal, self-confessional level as has been seen in *El pozo:* "I stroll through a well-kept, humid garden, my face receives the rain that does not explain anything, I think of distracted obscenities, I look at the glare on my parents' window. I do not want to learn to live, but to discover life once and for all" ("Paseo un jardín cuidado y húmedo, recibo en la cara la lluvia que nada explica, pienso distraídas obscenidades, miro el resplandor en la vantana de mis padres. No quiero aprender a vivir, sino descubrir la vida de una vez y para siempre.") (*oc*, 797)

The only notable difference between Eladio Linacero and Jorge Malabia is that possibly the latter might have a bit more fresh air, since Onetti transported his hero out of a single-cell habitat into a garden. The emotional commitment, the language, and the level of articulation, however, are identical. The rain and the well-kept garden are as indifferent, and incite the same apathy in the narrator-character as the furniture and unshaven face of Eladio Linacero did for him before.

The other narrative plane which comes from a removed, third person narrator is hardly a variant:

He was now disinterested, trying to blend in with the bottles, part of the others hardly out of curiosity. Díaz Grey's eyes met those of Marcos and he smiled. Sluggishly, more lame than ever, he moved closer to the bar, pulled over a stool and sat down next to the woman. Separated from the ground, his hands on his walking stick and covered by his hat, he felt at peace and resolved.

—San Martín—he said.

—Dry, doctor—the bartender concurred.

. . . .

—Good and dry, doctor—said the bartender placing the drink on the bar; he was looking and smiling at him; he had nothing to do with the other three by now, he was offering him a limitless complicity.

—Thank you—Díaz Grey mumbled; he drank down half of his drink and nodded.

Ahora estaba desinteresado, buscando confundirse con las botellas, apenas unido a los demás por su curiosidad. Díaz Grey encontró los ojos de Marcos y sonrió. Lentamente, más rengo que nunca, fue acercándose al mostrador, arrastró un taburete junto a la mujer y se sentó. Separado del suelo, las manos sobre el bastón y cubiertas por el sombrero, se sintió en paz y resuelto.

—San Martín—dijo.

—Seco, doctor—asintió el barman.

. . . .

—Bien seco, doctor—dijo el barman colocando la copa en el mostrador; lo miraba y le sonreía; ya nada tenía que ver con los otros tres, le estaba ofreciendo una complicidad sin límites.

—Gracias—murmuró Díaz Grey; bebió la mitad y dijo que sí con la cabeza. (*oc*, 840)

The focal point of this passage is Díaz Grey. The bartender is used as a kind of mirror for the objective recording of the scene that the narrator depicts; he mirrors the other characters and the conditions that define the atmosphere. Dr. Grey's actions and consciousness, that is, disinterest, withdrawal, "complicity," the motions of the other characters, the dialogue, and the narrator's record are all of one stylistic mold. The language does not vary; it is a laconic barroom language and depiction. The tone of feeling is complacent and indifferent. There is a unity within this scene which stylistically is as uniform as any of James' settings. Syntax, tone, scenery, motion, both physical and emotional, blend together as if the episode was being depicted by one man, the very same who is viewing and occupying the scene, a Linacero or Malabia. It is this kind of uniformity which led Emir Rodríguez-Monegal to say with reference to *Los adioses:* "The witness-narrator writes like Onetti,"[13] a statement which can be generalized to all of Onetti's narrators. The Uruguayan author is so insistent, so uniform in his stylistic elements that certainly some definite and firm ground offers itself for speculation on some possible reasons that underlie his particular idiolect. I think discussion of these possibilities might offer some concrete answers.

From the few passages already cited there is strong indication that Onetti has a certain affinity for a peculiar type of realism. It is, as the various narrators have demonstrated emphatically, a kind of poetic or subjective realism, a world portrayed in its crudity as it affects the psyche of the narrator or protagonist in the interplay of perception-expression with the object world. In this respect, then, it is a poetic, a personal realism offering a processed, subjective actuality. Insofar as this is true, Onetti is in the literary tradition of "naturalism," in which the object world occupies as significant a role as the psyches of the characters. In view of the role of geographical setting in Onetti's work, this is quite verifiable. However, Onetti's brand of realism, I should hasten to add, is more of the kind implied by the Brazilian writer Machado de Assis, who asserts that realism and reality are two completely different and separate entities. It is a kind of veracity operant in Joyce, Dos Passos, Sartre, Céline, and Faulkner; a "preciseness" which emanates from the subjective consciousness but has its foundation in the object-world of experience. Juan Carlos Onetti is as emphatic as one can be on this point in the fragment of the interview with Ms. Gilio cited above. Since it is in this tradition of "realism," Onetti's style is pretty much determined by an undisguised approach in his narrative. His style is basically the speaking style of his characters. Leonard Lutwack's observation on the realistic and naturalistic novel and its unique style is also applicable and serves to explain Onetti's stylistic peculiarity:

Since the naturalist takes no commanding view of his fiction, narrative and essay materials are presented in a style not far removed from the dull, unpointed speaking style of the characters, who are representatives of average humanity. The result is a monolithic dullness of language. In the later development of naturalism, however, the limitations of simple syntax and colorless diction become an intolerable burden, and we find naturalists resorting to a modified mixed style novel. By the use of "interchapters" that range in style from the newspaper headline to the stream of consciousness, Dos Passos sought ways of varying the uniform dullness of his prose and gaining access to subjective and even poetic expression.[14]

This passage from Lutwack contains succinctly a partial explanation of Onetti's narrative style and its development.

Unlike the naturalists of whom Lutwack is speaking here, however, Onetti has indeed taken a commanding view of his fiction from the very beginning. Eladio Linacero, his first protagonist-narrator, is depicted in the process of creating fiction. But as he tells us, it is a very special kind of story that he wishes to write: "I would like to write the story of a soul, all by itself."

Thus, from the very first, Onetti reaches for a poetic expression based on the subjective world. Even though Onetti is very much in the "realist-naturalist" tradition of Céline, Dos Passos, and Faulkner, like the last of these writers, his is the modified, poetic realism that Dos Passos and Steinbeck (in *Grapes of Wrath*) were able to attain. Their achievement is what Onetti has inherited.

La vida breve (1950) is perhaps the greatest stylistic achievement of Onetti in this respect, a work which proves to be much in the tradition of Dos Passos, Gide, and Céline. It utilizes with great effect the "interchapters" in the manner of Dos Passos, even more effectively than the cinematographic effects of *Tierra de nadie* which I will refer to shortly; it contains a masterful "commanding view" of fiction and the creation of fictional systems through the characters' fantasies. It demonstrates an acute grasp of the potential of man and his psyche to become "the other" and to create "the other" out of the stuff of Borgian dreams, and at the same time it reveals a brutal realism and naturalistic crudity matched only by the ruthless descriptions of Céline.

Nonetheless, the uniformity of style in Onetti is very prevalent. One might say, then, that the nature of the poetic expression which he introduces with *El pozo*, perfects with *El astillero*, and continues with *Juntacadáveres*, must have a cohesive oneness which gives it stylistic unity and uniformity throughout. At this point one begins to straddle style and content, the two spheres of medium and message. It is precisely here, on that meeting ground of definition and exercise, vision and portrayal, that we find the element which

gives Onetti's narrative and literary career a uniqueness and an un-
broken consistency. There is no essential change within this sphere
between *El pozo* and *Juntacadáveres* or *El astillero*. There is merely
a technical evolution and maturation in the construction of a fictional system. The materials used for this system, the foundation
which underlies the structure of this narrative, remains one and the
same. This constant is what we shall call Onetti's vision of reality
and of the world. Once again I refer to Lutwack, who explains the
relationship of uniform style to an author's vision of reality in these
terms: "Uniform style in a novel generally depends upon the
writer's settled conviction of the single unambiguous nature of his
materials and of the novel's adequacy as a vehicle for their serious
presentment. Insofar as style is a means of shutting out many possible views on a subject and directing attention to a few selected
views, a uniform style has the effects of better narrowing the scope
to a single, unified view of reality."[15]
Exactly what is this vision of reality to which Juan Carlos Onetti
is committed will become clearer as I discuss his modes of
characterization, his use of time and place, point of view, and the
evolution of his plots in the following chapters of this study.
Onetti's narrative, as already pointed out, unfolds basically on
two levels: that of a detached narrator recounting in the third person, and that of the unfolding of characters through sensations,
reactions, introspection, and afterthoughts. I have already
attempted to point out the striking parallel and similarity between
these two planes, and will return to this problem in my discussion of
narrative point of view. When the narrative, as in *El astillero*, comes
primarily from a detached third person narrator, insertions, or
"interchapters," break up the narrative. What is within these insertions is the subjective experience and individual consciousness of
the characters revealed to us in the first person. What constitutes
this consciousness are sensations, personal gestalts that are very individual and thus unique (Eladio Linacero's sensations, those of
Jorge Malabia, those of the witness-narrator in *Los adioses*). As
such, the idiolect or style of language of the consciousness being articulated is unique, personal, and of a poetic syntax. This poetic
syntax is Onetti's greatest stylistic achievement. His affinity for this
type of language is so great that even when he narrates in the
detached third person it is not difficult to notice that the man who
created the poesy in the language of a character's consciousness is

the same man behind the voice narrating the story, a fact which has led to wide criticism of Onetti on this point. This stylistic capability on the part of Onetti is what lends his narrative credibility. There are no paupers speaking in the language of kings. Since the narrative and fictional systems of Onetti have evolved into a closed cosmos geographically (Santa María), linguistically (*rioplatense*), and temporally (post - World War I), this kind of stylistic uniformity and credibility are crucial for maintaining the validity of that closed world, whether it be Eladio Linacero's room or Díaz Grey's Santa María, which the author has created and sealed off.

CHAPTER 2

The Shrouded Somnambulists: Onetti and Characterization

VIRGINIA Woolf has argued " . . . that all novels . . . deal with character, and that it is to express character—not to preach doctrines, sing songs, or celebrate the glories of the British Empire, that the form of the novel, so clumsy, verbose, and un- dramatic, so rich, elastic, and alive, has been evolved."[1] If we accept the emphatic significance that Woolf claims for the character in the novel, and I think we could indeed, very justifiably, then the manner of characterization is where the novelistic peculiarities of a writer are primarily revealed to us. As we have already seen in the cursory treatment of Juan Carlos Onetti's stylistic traits, the link between the author and his characters is so vital that it blends the realm of the two into a singular style of experience. If we take the art of the novel to be, like other forms of art, a manner of self- expression, it is where the gap is narrowest between creator and creation that we can unveil the greatest meaning with regard to the artist and the craftsmanship of his art. Onetti is not unique in this respect.

It is true of the genre of the novel as a whole that the artist often stands in the closest relation to his subject matter, as compared to other forms of art. This closeness of course should not be too sur- prising. The novelist deals with human beings and their world. As opposed to a composer who works with more abstract forms, therefore, there is a greater affinity between the novelist and his subject matter, which has a greater human density. This semblance is greater than ever in the contemporary novel. By contemporary, I mean novels since Proust, Joyce, and their inheritors of whom Juan Carlos Onetti is one of the most devout. It is precisely within the realm of this affinity, that hitherto neutral field between the artist and his creation, that the contemporary novel has made its greatest

headway, and it is within this sphere that the genre has found its
greatest innovation and the assurance of its perpetuity. This trend is
one very much tied to the subjectivism of the twentieth century.
The reader is no longer satisfied with an impersonal tale, delivered
to him impeccably in its final form. He demands that he be given
access to the artist's inner workings and to the process of the art's
formation. Consequently, the writer is constantly forced to expose
not only his work but himself as well. He can no longer remain aloof
and absent from his tale. The reader refuses to accept the hidden
presence of an omniscient creator and lives in what Nathalie
Saurraute calls "the age of suspicion," and no one is more aware of
this suspicion than the writer who speaks to his times.[2] For most
current novelists, even E. M. Forster's observations, that contain so
much truth, are no longer unquestionably sound. His comment that
a character in a book "is real when the novelist knows everything
about it"[3] seems to have little validity for today's novels and
authors. It is a product of great effort and viewed even as an accomplishment when a writer succeeds in conveying to the reader
that he knows no more than the reader about his characters, and
that he is watching them develop and unfold, just as the reader is
doing while reading the work. This, of course, introduces novelties
of drastic proportions into the technical elements of the art of the
novel, especially with regard to time and point of view. It means essentially the obliteration of the past perfect and of the removed
third-person perspective.

Juan Carlos Onetti is very much a part of this development. He
represents an early stage of it and is, in the case of the South
American writers, an initiator of this phenomenon and thus a
precursor to the most recent Latin American writers. From the very
beginning of Onetti's career we see his heroes and heroines reveal
themselves independently of their creator, with a culmination of
this tendency in *La vida breve* where the characters begin to create
themselves or each other. Onetti, the author, is allotted a menial
fleeting part inside his tale. He does not allow himself (or is not
allowed by his creatures) to rise above the reader's level of
awareness or the characters' existence. In a work like *Tierra de
nadie*, where the narrator is a detached voice recounting in the third
person, there is no attempt, even here, to depict the characters with
any background or antecedents. Only their present existence of that
moment in time is revealed to us. As Jaime Concha observes: "The
reader apprehends only actualized pasts and futures."[4]

The phenomenon of allowing the personages in fiction to evolve for themselves while both reader and writer look on is further emphasized in Onetti by the way in which we get acquainted with the characters, and what we learn about them upon our initial encounter with them.

The most direct and overt manner of presenting a character is through a name. It is the most traditional and most recurrent method. The way in which Onetti confronts this problem is aptly revealing of his peculiarities in characterization.

I *The Self-defining Character*

Beginning with *El pozo*, the protagonist speaks to us directly. This absolves the author from any responsibility. In the process of the narrative, however, we know little of the character other than the subjective sphere of his existence. His name he mentions for the first and last time in the second to the last paragraph of the novel.

In *Los adioses* we are only made aware of the names of the secondary characters. We know neither the name of the witness-narrator nor the names of the protagonist and the two women who are the central figures of Onetti's story.

The main characters of *Para una tumba sin nombre* are introduced no less inconspicuously. A couple of pages after the narrative is begun by a nameless witness-narrator, whom the initiated recognize as Dr. Díaz Grey, the main characters appear in a matter-of-fact way, casually in a conversation with the undertakers: " '. . . this Malabia boy, the younger one' "; " 'Rita García I believe, or González, single, an infarct, 35 years old, ruptured lungs. Do you understand?' " (*oc*, 990).

Even in a work where a case could be made for the absence of any protagonist or hero like *Tierra de nadie*, with as many characters as it has, none are introduced to us by the author by name. Often we have no idea about whom we are reading until a name casually falls from the mouth of another character in a dialogue. Especially in *Tierra de nadie*, the character's name, that convenient tag of identification, is always secondary to the description of that character and the setting around him. What particularly occupies the primary attention of the narrative voice is the subjective and inner state of being which emanates from the personages. It is especially through this focus on the realities of man's inner tumult that we derive our knowledge of the author's characters.

This technique, so frequent in Onetti, demonstrates both his contemporaneity and his sensitivity to the new trends of the novel. He is thus in the venerable tradition of Kafka, whose protagonist has no other name than the initial "K"; and of James Joyce whose hero in *Finnegan's Wake* is simply H. C. E.

Most of all, Onetti reflects the idiosyncrasies of his most immediate and acknowledged mentor, William Faulkner, and the ambiguities intentionally thrown into the reader's path, as in *The Sound and the Fury*, where two sets of characters go about with the same names of Quentin (the uncle and the niece), and Caddy (the mother and the daughter), or as with the happenstance name of Joe Christmas, the "hero" of *Light in August*.

This ambiguity in character identification ironically serves to illumine the reader more than the traditional clarity did. The absence of a name or the intentional muddling of it eliminates the possibility of the reader's too readily forming an impression on the identity of the character. In the absence of such a convenience, the reader is forced into a "complicity" with the author and must observe more closely the makeup of the characters in a novel. The operant factors determining the development of a character therefore become other than the *a priori* notions the reader ordinarily projects upon the identity of a personage.

The openness of mind resulting from the removal of this traditional crutch enables the writer to expose the characters' makeup in a way more faithful to his conception of the reality and essence of that figure. For a writer (like Faulkner, Juan Carlos Onetti, and Robbe-Grillet) who is attempting to portray a deeper reality, a more profound essence, psychological and "spiritual," through a special brand of realism, achievement of this is crucial. It was even more fundamental for writers at the turn of the century like Proust, Virginia Woolf, James Joyce, and Dorothy Richardson whose readers were still accustomed to the ready-made character identities of the nineteenth-century novel. This might explain what then seemed to be drastic measures. In works where the writer has most nearly achieved the conveyance of this inner subjective or psychological reality, the hero's name is an obscure entity, a collectors' item for students of literature. The question has been asked before, how many people remember the name of Camus' hero in *L'Etranger?* In the same vein we might inadvertently ask, Who is the hero of Onetti's *Tierra de nadie* or of *Los adioses?*

The technique of portrayal discussed so far and adhered to by

Onetti is in keeping with his overall aesthetics of characterization and with the nature of the human beings he attempts to render. The emphasis is invariably on the inner psyche of the character. We are not given Eladio Linacero's name until the end of the novel, or we might not know anything about the birth, childhood, or adolescence of a Junta Larsen, but we do have a comprehension of the protagonists' spiritual essence, their subjective turmoil, fantasies, and psychological convulsions.

In keeping with this purpose of depicting humanity from within, Onetti's characters can only be seen and solely expose themselves through their subjective experience. This might account for Onetti's never abandoning narration through the "I," the first-person interlocutor, even in the novels of third-person narration. Thus, the accurateness of Jaime Concha's statment: "the characters are not aware of anything except their precise field of subjective experience."[5] Since there is no interference on the part of the author, what the reader observes is precisely this cognizance of the characters' subjective experience.

While Juan Carlos Onetti is deeply involved in using the devices of characterization prevalent in the contemporary novel, we should also note that like his contemporaries he is aware of the newly expanded power that an author has over his fictional system and its characters. In other words, we should not lose sight of the fact that even though Juan María Brausen created Arce and fantasized Díaz Grey, it is Onetti who has created Brausen and embued him with the power to create others. The point to be made is that it would be a misconception on our part to assume that because the character of the modern novel is seemingly given the utmost autonomy and independence by his creator, the latter has less omniscience than before. The recourse is a matter of technique for producing a literature more in keeping with the psychic consensus of the epoch. Even Nathalie Saurraute's antinovel novels and her anticharacter characters are products of an author's imagination that wields a pen and gives "life" to the antihero. Literature is art and as such emanates from the creative imagination and its intention. If a character were able to come into being and exist by himself he would have no need of the writer, and finally would cease to be an emanation from art and become a phenomenon of the everyday world, just like every one of us. It should also be noted that because we are made aware of a more profound reality, and the characters of a novel reveal themselves at greater subjective and psychological depths, the consciousness and awareness level of the writer are proportionally more intense. The author's technical skill is obviously as great, since it has become necessary for us to reassure ourselves as to who created whom. (This becomes reminiscent of Pirandello's *Six Characters in Search of an Author* or Unamuno's *Niebla*.) With no intention of plunging into paradoxes, one could say that commensurate with the autonomy that a contemporary writer like Onetti grants his characters, the power he wields over them is increased. He has access to greater recesses of the characters' inner world, just as we do as his readers.

Interestingly enough, the criticism of Juan Carlos Onetti's work focuses on this phenomenon, and seems to be unanimously in agreement that the author's characters have no autonomy whatsoever. Luis Harss is under the impression that there is only a semblance of autonomy for the characters in *Los adioses;* Mario Benedetti and James Irby link Onetti to Faulkner and to the fatality of time, the past predetermining any existence in the present or future; Jaime Concha considers Onetti an embalmer of his personages, halting them in their existence; Caracé Hernández sees Onetti's characters as "instruments or demiurgical personifications, without any glitter of their own."[6] All of these critics have also unanimously failed to point out what or who it is that deprives the Onettian characters of their autonomy. The nature of their statements seems to indicate that they confuse Onetti the craftsman with the vision of the world and the nature of a reality that Onetti happens to believe in and by which he is governed. As I have tried to demonstrate, Onetti the writer is most generous in his willingness to give his characters a vast autonomy and independence before the reader. As a craftsman of characterization, he accomplishes this liberation for his characters. What deprives them of the human freedom that these critics miss is the nature of reality, they way of the world that Onetti is committed to. Because he is able to infuse his personages with a sense of futile liberty which taunts the human predicament, Onetti is a successful writer. Technically he manages to characterize his personages with an air of freedom which at times reaches an exasperating degree of "indifference" and all-pervasive pathos. Contrasted with this technical recourse that some critics overlook is a vision of reality which is devastatingly fatalistic and obliterates all possibility for human freedom, canceling every likelihood of choice, self-determination, or chance in the future. This dialectic in the work of Onetti is both aesthetically and philosophically at the heart of his vision as an artist. Through this dialectic the author expresses the existential predicament of modern man: the impossibility of human autonomy or freedom. It is this fatality that subjugates and dominates Onetti's characters, as well as Onetti himself.

II *Method and Message*

The distinction must be made between the method or technique of characterization and the human condition of the characters as a metaphor for man's predicament. The relationship between these two aspects of a work should also be kept always in mind by those who sincerely aspire to an understanding of a work and the cosmos of a writer.

There is no question about it; the fate of the characters that populate Onetti's fictional world is laden with a futility and choked desperation which results in an attitude of disinterest and indifference, or somnolent fantasizing on the part of these characters, the latter perhaps being the sole saving factor which intervenes between life and death. Insofar as Onetti is subject to his own vision of human reality, he has equated himself and his own fate to that of his characters.

The hero of his first novel, Eladio Linacero, proclaims the fate of the Onettian man when he tells us, "I am a solitary man that smokes in any old place of the city; the night surrounds me, it fulfills itself like a rite, gradually, and I have nothing to do with it" (*oc*, 75). As Mario Benedetti points out, none of Onetti's subsequent protagonists cease being that solitary man, whose obsession is to contemplate how life surrounds them without their having anything to do with it.[7]

This lot of Onetti's characters has its source in the fortune of the author himself and the circumstances which forced him to create these personages. Onetti's own life is one of almost total absence from the world and those around him. According to Luis Harss, "it was this physical and emotional isolation, he has said, that turned him into a writer in the first place, in spite of himself, for unknown reasons out of habit."[8] With such a point of departure it is inevitable that Onetti's heroes should be fated to endure the solitude and alienation which characterize their creator, and in his tenet, every modern man. This conviction is what destines all of the inhabitants of Onetti's fictional world to a similar fate. His brand of fatality, therefore, comes to be generic, irrespective of individual destinies and paths of life. With such an inevitable fate, the future for Onetti's characters is clearly defined and holds no surprises. Where men differ for Onetti, as for William Faulkner, is in their past, the past which irrevocably draws each one to the common end of solitude, alienation, misunderstanding, and death. Both James Irby and Mario Benedetti have pointed out that the unknown variable in this algebraic equation with a constant resolution, is the past. Unlike the traditional order, the resolution itself is given before the unknown elements of the problem are presented. The narrative of Onetti is comprised of reconstructing the problemata which yield the resolution. Thus, beginning with Eladio Linacero, we turn back to the youth, adolescence, and childhood of the character until by the end of the novel we reach the actual moment of narration with which the story begins. The sequel novels, *El astillero* and *Juntacadáveres*, function in the same manner. In *El astillero* (1961) we witness the fatal end of Junta Larsen; in *Juntacadáveres*, (1964) we view the reconstruction of the events of five years earlier which led to this end. As in the stylistic structure of *El pozo*, we see a closed circular system, a vicious cycle at that, with no way out. The fact that at every point of articulation in Onetti's literary career, with each new novel, we have to return to his first work in order to relate to his fictional system, and to grasp its expanding perimeter, is also an emphatic indication of the circularity.

It is in this strong umbilical tie to the past that William Faulkner has had the greatest influence on Onetti. Sartre's evaluation of the American writer, as related by R. W. B. Lewis, suits Onetti perfectly: "Faulkner wrote . . . as though man were completely without a future, possessed only of a past; but he should write *as though* man might have a future. The glance was all backward in Faulkner; and human life . . . appeared as a road watched despairingly as it flowed away, from the rear window of a moving car."[9]

III *The Everpresent Past and Precluded Freedom*

Within the confines of such a straightjacket, of a past sealed by the fatality of a predictable end, we observe the characters of Onetti in a cycle of inane gesticulations. The helplessness engendered by such circumstances becomes the only impetus for the characters' continued survival. And yet, despite the similar nature of the fate which they share, Onetti's characters find it impossible to achieve a human communion that can ease or free them from the clutches of an oppressive solitude and alienation. Thus the fatality of these quarantined destinies becomes even more tyrannical. In the end it all turns into a complacent nightmare, complacent because eventually each personage realizes the futility of action and thus falls back into an irrevocable state of passive resignation.

In certain works this oppressive tyranny is depicted in more than symbolic terms. *Para esta noche* (1943) portrays a city literally under siege. The novel, with its alternating perspectives which present the same situation from the point of view of the antagonist as well as that of the protagonist, is basically the story of man imprisoned within the city by a ruthless military siege. As the circumstances entrap the hero and his companions, the intensity of the situation builds up, only to reach a denouement of futility and death. In this third major work by the author there is a last desperate gesture toward the end of the novel at action and human communion, which accentuates this futility to its utmost. The protagonist, Ossorio and, ironically enough, Victoria, meet their brutal and inescapable fate. It is an unheroic end devoid of the last vestiges of human communion, initiative, or dignity. Though circumstantially this last scene of *Para esta noche* is similar to that memorable episode of André Malraux's *La Condition Humaine*, it lacks the heroism demonstrated by those doomed human creatures who attempt to take death into their own hands by sharing, with dignity, a cyanide tablet.

Freedom of choice and individual initiative does not exist for Onetti, either in life or in the face of death. And even if man appears to act out of self-initiative, that freedom is still within the bounds and dictates of a predetermining fate; it is of no use. This sentiment reaches its culmination in Onetti's *El astillero*, a work which is the portrayal of an end, a symphony of human futility conducted by Fate and performed by Junta Larsen as well as by Juan Carlos Onetti.

Junta Larsen has a distinguished career as a character in Onetti's cosmogony. *El astillero* is both the apotheosis and nadir of this protagonist. Leaving his failures behind, Junta Larsen undertakes the management of a defunct shipyard, owned by the demented Jeremías Petrus, and for a time participates in the ideal (madness, self-delusion) of resuscitating the derelict. In the end, this final undertaking proves to be a parting gesture, a flight into the face of the inevitable and inexorable fate of those characters who attempt to counter the Onettian vision of destiny. As this realization dawns on Junta Larsen, this is the way in which it is articulated:

> Larsen pushed the files aside and went over to the window to stick one hand and then the other into the fog. "It just can't be," he kept repeating. He would have preferred an earlier date, a more youthful time for what was about to happen: he would have preferred another type of faith to do it: "But they never let one choose, only afterward does one realize that he might have chosen." He stroked the trigger of the gun under his arm while he listened to the harshness of silence. . . . (*oc*, 1101 - 2)

What we come to realize along with Larsen is that a man cannot even choose his own death in Onetti's world. As this character admits shortly after this realization, "There are no surprises in life, you are right; at least for real man. We know it by memory, like a woman, if I may say so. And as far as life's meaning, don't think that I am talking in vain. I understand a bit. One does things, but cannot do other than what he does. Or, in other words, one can't always choose" (*oc*, 1117).

As if this painful awareness were not sufficient, Juan Carlos Onetti goes a step further in tantalizing the consciousness, Larsen's, ours, and his own by positing two alternative endings to the novel and to Larsen. Onetti proceeds as if it mattered one way or another, knowing full well that it does not. Yet he insists on dangling a fruitless alternative before the reader's and his characters' eyes. This is not a novelty with *El astillero*, for the same occurs at the end of *La vida breve*. Though it might seem redundant, the technique is effective. It reassures everyone that it cannot happen any other way but in the way that it has actually occurred, and even if it should happen differently, the end result is always the same: defeat and death.

In the face of such a fateful impasse, Onetti's characters respond in the same way that their creator has chosen to face this futile human condition, by turning to the sphere of fantasy, the dream world, the realm of creative imagination. Thus, in the same way that Onetti creates the fictitious world of these figures, they in turn invent theirs by resorting to fantasies and to the imagination, to the world of make-believe, and to a reality which seemingly differs from that of their human condition and from that of our daily lives. Once again, Onetti's characters and fictional cosmos are an ectoplasm of himself. Very much like Proust, Juan Carlos Onetti puts his faith in art, in human creativeness, and in the capacity of man to transcend the predicament of his worldly existence through his inventions. There is only one marked difference between Proust and Onetti, however. Whereas Proust succeeds or feels that he succeeds in transcending the ephemerality of human existence, Onetti transposes the fatality of the human condition to the realm of artistic creation, to the imaginary. As we see in *El pozo, La vida breve*, and *El astillero*, man temporarily and in fleeting moments manages to console himself through his fantasy. But in the long run, even within this sphere of the imagination, the futility haunts the end of man and reduces him to no different a finality from that of his original existence which he sought to escape. And even while in the process of fantasy and dissimulation, Onetti's men are fully cognizant of their chimera, as is *El pozo*'s Eladio Linacero: "I am a poor man who, in the night, turns to face the shadows on the wall and think of fantastic and absurd things" (*oc*, 74). Or with Dr. Díaz Grey of *El astillero*: "Everyone knowing that our way of life is a farce, capable of admitting it, but not doing so because each of us needs to protect a personal farce besides. I also, of course" (*oc*, 1118).

Díaz Grey's statement attests to what "Jeremías Petrus, Sociedad Anónima" represents to the human beings the author placed in this desolate mooring. Through Díaz Grey's statement, then, the work signifies a double make-believe.

Along with the stylistic uniformity, another constant which is omnipresent in Onetti's work is the evocation of the oneiric. Through a realism which recognizes that the makeup of every human psyche is partially constituted and nourished by dreams and the imagination, Onetti manages to transport the reader to the realm of the characters' fantasy world. For Onetti the realist, the oneiric world is just as real as the concrete world of his and his characters' existence. We can conclude that for Onetti, the world of his fiction is as real as the reality in which he carries on his daily activities. From the very beginning of Onetti's fiction we see an interwoven pattern comprised of the oneiric and the concrete, what we can rightfully call a "complete" reality, the reality which is the existence and human condition of the men and women who populate Onetti's world.

IV   *Lost Souls*

The realms of dream or fantasy in Onetti's work constantly multiply in the progression of his career. The multiplication is in direct proportion to the increase in the "realities" or characters within his fictional system. Whereas in *El pozo* there is only a single "reality," that of Eladio Linacero, and thus a single fantasy world, in *Tierra de nadie* this phantasmal sphere multiplies to correspond to each "reality" operating in the work: that of Aránzuru, of Casal, of Nora, of Balbina, of Ernesto, of Llarvi, of Nené, of Mauricio Offen, of Demetrio Sata, of Martín, of Samuel Rada, of Violeta, and last but not least, that of Pablo Num, the embalmer. We of course should not forget to add to the list one last "reality" to which each one of these is inextricably tied, that of Juan Carlos Onetti himself that engenders all the rest.

Onetti's second novel is in the tradition of those works which are a part of every national literature and which attempt to capture a quintescence of a national character, a mode of being within a society in a given time. *Tierra de nadie* is in this respect Onetti's version of Joyce's *Dubliners*, Sherwood Anderson's *Winesburg Ohio*, Dos Passos' *Manhattan Transfer*, Döblin's *Berlin Alexanderplatz*. The roster of characters is an embodiment of Buenos Aires. They are Buenos Aires. They are the "wandering rocks" of *Ulysses* in their River Plate rendition. It is difficult to distill a synopsis of Onetti's second work for the simple reason that nothing happens in it. The novel is precisely about what does not happen, about the impossibility of anything coming from this lost generation of alienated city dwellers who exist on their individual and individuated "realities" that are more oneiric than real. *Tierra de nadie* is a kaleidoscope of disjointed human elements that float in the impure sea of a modern urbanity. Occasionally these disparate elements coincide, enjoin superficially, primarily through the shallow contact of epidermises, and then disengage once again, retreating to face the complicated consequences of social existence now made more perplexing by the inanity apparent in the incidental contact. The work itself has no unity, nor do the lives and the social "order" it depicts. While the characters can be viewed as alienated, marginal elements estranged from society, in reality they *are* society, they are the city. They are the disoriented, amoral, indifferent mass of failures, daydreamers, utopians, men and women who are sustained by the power of their fantasies. On a more symbolic plane, the city these personages represent is itself marginal to the world, estranged from the human struggle of a world across the Atlantic in the throes of war, in a desperate battle of survival. A way of life, a world view, the very foundations on which the New World was founded are being threatened as Buenos Aires must look on from the distance. With the multiplicity of dreams, and the inevitable contact between the somnambulists, whose only visible ligature is through the flesh and the sexual act, there arises, to use Jaime Concha's phrase, "the possibility of the shared dream,"[10] the potentiality of a world whose inhabitants coexist at the oneiric plane through a series of shared dreams and fantasies.

In effect, the possibility does not remain a mere possibility. Through the oneiric and the imagination we see for the first time certain bonds forming between Onettian characters. Casal, the aspiring artist, creates a painting depicting monstrous and deformed lepers. The motif of Casal's lepers corresponds to a dream of Nené. This coincidence between the dream of the woman and the artistic figures of Casal creates a kind of bond between the two characters.

The greatest bond which emanates from fantasy, however, is through the dreamed island, a figment of old Num's imagination invented as an inheritance for Nora, his daughter. For the characters involved, this dream takes on the proportions of actual reality in which they come to believe. Aránzuru, the lawyer who is managing the affairs of Nora's inheritance, legalizes the dream and makes it official through his public position. Num thus confesses to Aránzuru: "Well, Aránzuru. You are philosophical. See how curious. . . . Because, I had invented the inheritance for her, so that the girl would be happy. And she goes and invents it so I can be happy, and I pretend that I believe it . . . " (*oc*, 99).

The inheritance-dream shared and sustained by the characters in the novel is an island, Faruru. Interestingly enough, twenty years later, and as many years after Aránzuru's suicide and *Tierra de nadie*, Juan Carlos Onetti still vicariously nourishes the illusion of the institutionalized dream; there is mention in *El astillero* of an island near the port of Santa María which housed "el palacio de Latorre" and to which Jeremías Petrus aspired. We are informed, however, that Petrus was not able to acquire his dream palace: "It was decided behind destiny's back to declare the Latorre palace a historical monument, to buy it for the nation and to pay a salary to a substitute professor of national history to live there and report regularly on leaks, threatening weeds, and the dialogue between the tides and the solidity of the foundations. The professor's name, although it is now immaterial, was Aránzuru. They said that he used to be a lawyer but he no longer was one" (*oc*, 1135).

Aránzuru's fleeting apparition in the dream or nightmare world, whose chief protagonist is Junta Larsen, complies with Onetti's rules of reciprocity in the sphere of the oneiric, and to the author's undying dedication to his characters' dreams. Junta Larsen makes a similar fleeting appearance in *Tierra de nadie* when he is invited by Aránzuru to accompany him to the Nums' imaginary island. At the time, Larsen's response is, "It's better to go rut in any old place" ("Más vale irse a pudrir a cualquiera parte") (*oc*, 234).

It would appear that dreams are not simply the bond among characters only within a given novel of Onetti, but rather the ligature and cohesive element which runs through and unifies all of his work. This phenomenon is most emphatically manifest in Onetti's intentional and willing attempt to *create* within the realm of the dreamed and oneiric inventions of his characters. The tendency reaches its culmination with *La vida breve* and with the creation of the mythical Santa María. It should be noted, therefore, that dreams do not only function as the communion ground of Onetti's characters, but they also occasion a bond between Onetti himself, his characters, and their world. Jaime Concha has scribbled a very appropriate annotation in the margins of his lecture notes on Onetti which he delivered at La Universidad de Concepción, Chile in 1966 that I would like to include here: "Onetti speaks of a fate of transcendence (he does not use that word) through the creation of characters. . . . Better yet—he says that the author *loses* himself in his characters in order to *save* himself. He cites the scriptures: those who wish to save themselves will face perdition."

By his fourth novel, *La vida breve*, it seems that Onetti and his heroes are convinced that the only answer to the human condition lies in the realm of the oneiric and the world of fantasy. Both the author and his characters seek their salvation, then, and are irrevocably convinced of their lot within the realm of the imagination. Though Onetti stylistically is still a "realist," as are his heroes in "imitation" of their creator, the realism is transposed to a world of fantasy. Given the assimilation of these elements (realism, imagination, and the oneiric), it is inevitable that a mundane cosmos with all its trite details should emerge in the dream world. This, of course, is the world of Santa María and all of its inhabitants and their lore, all emanating from the tormented life of solitude, alienation, and the fertile imagination of Juan María Brausen of *La vida breve*.

Juan María Brausen is a key character in Juan Carlos Onetti's

literary gallery: as an alienated, solitary human being, he reflects
Onetti's vision of man; as a man who finds his condition in the
world oppressive and turns to the world of fantasy, to the creation of
other worlds and other "selves," he reflects Onetti himself; as a
creative human being who invents a cosmos and projects his own
existence into it, a cosmos which would provide a setting to his
creator's subsequent "fantasies," he *is* Onetti himself. Brausen
represents an incarnation of the poetics and metaphysics of Onetti;
the poetics of the dreamworld and the metaphysics of subjectivity,
the inner self as the only realm in which man can find his salvation.
Through Brausen, the author is reasserting the belief that man's
salvation is to be found precisely within that terrain of solitude and
the solitary self from which man seeks to transcend. Since we are
equating literature with the oneiric and the imaginative inventions
(writing literature with dreaming) an Uruguayan critic's statement
about Onetti and his heroes is apt here: "it is solitude that generates
the imperious necessity to write. One is a writer when he is in absolute solitude."[11]
Alienation appears to be all-pervasive within the Onettian
metaphysics. The problem put before us and his protagonists is,
Can there be salvation through perdition, as Onetti seeks for
himself according to Jaime Concha, or as his protagonists' predicament implies; can man escape alienation through solitude, through
self-consciousness and reliance on the subjective, oneiric fantasy
world?

V   *Pathetic Impasse*

Neither the author nor his characters seem to be very optimistic
in this quest. There are two explicit moments in Juan Carlos Onetti's career, and a myriad of implicit ones (the author's entire work is
a metaphor for this problem), in which he and his protagonists
overtly reflect on the metaphysics of this predicament. One is in
Tierra de nadie and the other in *La vida breve*.
In *Tierra de nadie*, Llarvi is by far the most acutely intellectual of
all the characters. Onetti utilizes Llarvi, in a very Gide-like manner,
as a touchstone for certain technical recourses: as an indication of
time, as a consciousness which reflects the human predicament of
all the characters. Llarvi is useful in this way mainly for his journal.
As Edouard in *Les Faux Monneyeurs*, he is a mirror of his creator.
In the end, at the age of thirty-five, Llarvi, disillusioned with life

and his own subjectivity, does away with himself. Prior to this finality, however, in an undated entry in his journal, he musters the
courage, or indifference, to offer a summation of his own awareness
with regard to human existence. Very keenly aware of the potential
of that moment when man can feel free and unabashed to speak as
honestly and as sincerely as he can at no other time, Llarvi offers his
résumé of the human experience through the description of his
relationship with Labuk, an early involvement of shadowy psychological implications. The Chilean critic Jaime Concha sums up
the implications of Llarvi's last entry into his journal in this fashion:
"With an analysis that hangs halfway between being cold and
pathetic, Llarvi has been able to pinpoint three instances within the
process of self awareness: the forsaking of all that is social, the consciousness of one's own flesh, and the experience of the deceitful
nothingness of the inner being."[12] At the moment of this articulation, Llarvi finds himself suspended (like Carlos Fuentes' Artemio
Cruz) between being and nonbeing, in that Rilkean twilight which
borders on both sleep and wakefulness. We can attribute the
acuteness and clarity of his final analysis to the magical quality of
this moment when nothing is at stake and everything hangs in the
balance. The potential of his dictum being applicable to the entire
work of his creator, connotes that Llarvi is echoing the sentiments of
Onetti himself.

The other instance in Onetti's career in which the question of
redemption and the possibility of salvation through oneiric invention is taken up occurs in *La vida breve*. The principal leitmotiv of
La vida breve is the novelistic development and the unfolding of
precisely the *summa vitae* that Llarvi leaves to posterity in *Tierra de
nadie*. The novel's protagonist, Juan María Brausen ("legitimate
descendent of Eladio Linacero," according to Emir Rodríguez-
Monegal),[13] embarks on an odyssey which is the incarnation of what
Llarvi, in his final moment of illumination, relates almost as a
posthumous afterthought.

Brausen, husband, bureaucrat, and member of the respectable
and responsible urban bourgeoisie views his world of responsibility
and respectable existence with a repugnance bordering on revulsion
which has become an obsession. Through the wall of his apartment
he listens to the occurrencas of another world. This shady world of
the adjoining apartment becomes the mechanism and the alternative through which he discards his own identity; it becomes both
the mode and the end of his "social catharsis." In this new world

and new life Juan María Brausen becomes Arce, existing concurrently, simultaneously yet separate and distinct, from Brausen. As Rodríguez-Monegal points out, the world of Brausen is one of responsibility and routine, while that of Arce is one of escape.[14] Interestingly enough, as if Llarvi has sketched for Onetti the work which was to follow *Tierra de nadie,* the novel begins with Brausen standing naked after a shower, conscious of his wet flesh and the water droplets on his skin while he listens to the woman through the wall and trys to reconstruct the world implicit in the woman's talk. Simultaneously, Brausen reflects, and in a stream-of-consciousness monologue which typifies Onetti's confessor-narrators, articulates his feelings and thoughts about his wife Gertrudis' scarred body. The horrid descriptions of her abdomen and her amputated left breast intensely attest to Brausen's "consciousness of one's flesh" to use Llarvi's terminology.

Brausen, in addition to this new, other identity and life he adopts, seeks refuge from his humdrum, senseless existence in the realm of fantasy. There is a cinematographic plot (a script he is supposed to be writing for the agency in which he is employed) that he recurrently evokes as an obsession and which, as we have since come to know it, is the world of Santa María, the realm of the Onettian saga. Brausen's involvement in this imaginary realm is as complete as is his involvement in his lives as Brausen and Arce. There is only one difference between the world of the imagined and the other two lives. Unlike the latter two, the existence in this fantasy emanates from the deep recesses of Brausen's subjectivity and inner private world. Thus, Brausen is now potentially on the verge of fulfilling the third step of Llarvi's dictum: "the experience of the deceitful nothingness of the inner being." Effectively, as it turns out, this potential is fulfilled as it was articulated by Llarvi. In the fictitious world of Santa María and Díaz Grey, its first and most distinguished denizen, Brausen discovers that the human condition cannot transcend the existential predicament of misunderstanding, senselessness, routine, and surfeit that plague man in his daily existence. The world that he has created for his "protagonist," Díaz Grey, ends up being "a transparent stylization of the reality that oppresses Brausen."[15] This outcome may well be symbolic of Onetti's own predicament as he himself envisions it. Perhaps it might be his assessment of his own chances of achieving *salvation* through *perdition,* that is, through the loss of self in the world of his characters.

Returning to Brausen and his imaginary creations, we see that as

the imagined cosmos of Díaz Grey takes on the lineaments of a
world unto itself, life there too becomes a sordid affair. By the end
of the novel this becomes quite convincing, and we see both Onetti
and Brausen also believing that the reality of man resides both
within and without him, and that he carries this reality wherever he
ventures, whether it be into the escapist world of dreams or into the
structured realm of the creative imagination. The last chapter of *La
vida breve* entitled "El señor Albano" leaves no doubt as to the self-
deception and disillusionment in which the inner, subjective self
finds itself in the final analysis. Life as depicted here is a masquerade, each man as isolated and misunderstood as in the world of
Brausen the bureaucrat or Arce the "criminal." In a sentence of the
novel, which is both an assessment of the events of this work and
the entire *oeuvre* of Juan Carlos Onetti, it is all summed up in this
manner: "Nothing is interrupted, nothing ends; even though the
myopics are thrown off the track with the change of circumstances
and characters" ("Nada se interrumpe, nada termina; aunque los
miopes se despisten con los cambios de circunstancias y personajes") (*oc*, 709).

Interestingly enough, it is not only the humdrum world of
Brausen that fuses into the world of Díaz Grey and Santa María, but
the world of Arce, his alter ego, is involved as well. Fleeing with the
murderer Ernesto who committed the murder he himself was
meditating, Arce-Brausen seeks refuge in the imagined Santa
María. The flight, however, is desperate. Even in this imaginary
world they must seek disguises. Thus, Brausen, who was forced to
look for another identity and found that of Arce, is once again in
that same predicament. This is why the novel concludes in the
imaginary world of Santa María at a masquerade in which
"—escape, salvation, the future that unites us and which only I can
remember—is dependent on our not making a mistake while choos-
ing the disguise" (*oc*, 696). Even the disguise, however, proves
futile in the end, for this is the same voice which sixteen pages later
will say, "Nothing is interrupted, nothing ends; even though the
myopics are thrown off track by changes of circumstances and
characters" ("Nada se interrumpe, nada termina; aunque los
miopes se despisten con los cambios de circunstancias y personajes").

Brausen's wishful statement is now futile: "This is what I was
looking for from the very beginning, since the death of the man that
lived for five years with Gertrudis; to be free, irresponsible toward

others, to conquer myself without a struggle in true solitude" (*oc*, 694). The outcome of his longed-for liberty, of "the self-conquest in solitude," has led to the same impasse as that which the Brausen, who lived with Gertrudis for five years, had to confront. Brausen never really liberated himself as a result of discarding his old life and identity. It is as if, during all of this time since he became Arce and Brausen of Santa María, he were standing still. For in the stroke of one moment and one utterance he is flung back to the old Brausen he abandoned. When he finds himself in Santa María and the thought just cited is in the process of going through his mind, he is told, "You are the other. . . . Then you are Brausen" ("Usted es el otro. . . . Entonces usted es Brausen") (*oc*, 694) a statement which returns him to the time prior to Arce, prior to Díaz Grey and Santa María. It is all an emphatic reminder that despite his fantasy, his new identity, his "self-liberation," he never ceased to be what he was: Juan María Brausen, bourgeois, husband, bureaucrat, a slave to the boredom, routine, and misunderstanding of a senseless existence.

In the end Brausen realizes that he is a nobody, a mere incarnation of Juan María Brausen. He thus has come full circle, back to the starting point. Whether he be Brausen in Buenos Aires, or reincarnated as Díaz Grey in Santa María, his lot as a man is the same, no better in the world of the "imaginary" than in the world of "reality." Once again Onetti's implication is that there is no difference between the real and the imaginary; the first is as real or as unreal as the second. One thing is certain, however, that in both an inevitable futility awaits man.

La vida breve, then, may be said to be a crucial midpoint in Onetti's career as artist and metaphysician. All works prior to it (*El pozo, Tierra de nadie, Para esta noche*) contain the implicit elaborations of the metaphysics that becomes overtly manifest both in the content and form of *La vida breve*. All other major works which follow this crucial midpoint (*Los adioses, Para una tumba sin nombre, El astillero, Juntacadáveres, La muerte y la niña*) have as their fundamental construct *La vida breve*, which is their springboard. We need cite only one factor to justify this claim. Of the works here named as subsequent to *La vida breve*, only *Los adioses* stands apart from the rest in terms of characterization. All the other works have in common a world and its inhabitants which emanate from Juan María Brausen's oneiric subjectivity: Santa María and its people.

By adapting Brausen's fantasy into the official world of literature, Juan Carlos Onetti once again evokes the phenomenon of "the shared dream" ("el sueño compartido") which we witness in *Tierra de nadie*. Only now Aránzuru is Onetti himself, sanctioning and sharing the dream of Brausen. Thus, the familiar figures of Dr. Díaz Grey, Junta Larsen, Jorge Malabia, Father Bergner, Jeremías Petrus, and among them denizens of shorter works like Jacob Van Otto and Prince Orsini of "Jacob y el otro," all are the offspring of that dream shared by Juan María Brausen and Juan Carlos Onetti. In the end, however, as with *El pozo* and Eladio Linacero, even though the oneiric and fantasy world has refracted and multiplied, the outcome is the same indifferent destiny which carries everyone and everything "inexorably downstream"; man's fate, like the night which surrounds Linacero, "fulfills itself as a rite" irrespective of dreams, poesy, wishes, or gesticulation of the men which convulse in it. All of which is quite reminiscent of Jean Paul Sartre's comment concerning John Dos Passos: "The lives he tells about are all closed in on themselves. They resemble those Bergsonian memories which, after the body's death, float about, lifeless and full of odours and lights and cries, through some forgotten limbo. We constantly have the feeling that these vague human lives are destinies."[16]

The "body's death" that Sartre speaks of is as crucial in Onetti's narrative as in that of Dos Passos. This brings us to another juncture of misunderstanding between Onetti and his critics. What is frequently referred to as Onetti's obsession with the sexual relationships between his characters is not precisely an obsession in itself, but rather a necessary manifestation of a more encompassing preoccupation with the human body. In the final analysis, as I have attempted to demonstrate, Onetti's man exists in his own inner world, and he manifests himself from that interior. As I also pointed out, however, and as Sartre asserts with respect to Dos Passos, Onetti's narrative process of revealing is itself a "hybrid," the duality arising from the characters being introspective, introverted, and confessional, thus functioning in the realm of the subjective, and from the realism which marks the narrative of Onetti himself. This realism is at the heart of the author's preoccupation with the body and the corporal, of which the sexual is inherently a part. Moreover, Onetti's attempt to depict a kind of human being who lives *within* is also necessarily a cause for his constant obsession with the body. To achieve the purely subjective, it is imperative to obliterate the objective, the vulgar, the anatomical, which hinders a type of existence that Onetti is attempting to portray: the existence of the characters' inner recesses, or that inner world which is the character. Thus, the Onettian cosmos is a series of bodily negations which begins with Eladio Linacero's nausea over his body and his ill-fated corporal relationship with Ana María and later with Cecilia Huerta, and ends with Junta Larsen's revulsion toward the pregnant belly of Gálvez's woman. Between these two chronological points is another series of bodily and sexual entanglements which imply the disillusionment for the men and perdition of the women: in *Tierra de nadie,* Nené abandoned by Aránzuru, and Nora violated by Larsen; in *Para esta noche,* the ill-fated flight of Ossorio with Barcala's daughter; in *La vida breve,* Brausen's nausea and disgust with his wife's body, and also his youthful adventure with Raquel; to say nothing of the sordid entanglements in *Para una tumba sin nombre* and *Juntacadáveres* which will be discussed shortly. I shall develop further the theme of innocence and experience, innocence-purity and puberty-disillusionment, in the female character especially, in my discussion of character change as a function of plot in Onetti's work.

It is readily apparent that one of the greatest impetuses for the characters' flight into the subjective, oneiric, inner fantasy world is precisely the negative and repugnant confrontation with the sordid bodily and objective existence. This is, after all, precisely one of the three stages on the path to self-awareness and self-realization that Llarvi posits in *Tierra de nadie:* "consciousness of one's own flesh." The phrase implies more than just one's own body; it implies bodily existence in general which surrounds one and gives a definition to the flesh and objective dimensions of one's own self, whether it be through the sexual act or through the imposing sight of an overripe pregnancy in hemorrhage. Thus, the bodily and the objective are as necessary to the subjective and to the oneiric as is reality to the imagination or death to life. It is, as Sartre would have it, an "antivalue."[17]

CHAPTER 3

Cells and Fragmented Eternity: Time and Place in Onetti's Work

A T the outset of Onetti's career, the rudiments of time and place furnish the requisite elements for a straightjacket. These two elemental dimensions function as an oppressive force whose insufferable weight compels the author's narrators and characters to seek, not unlike their creator, an escape in the oneiric and somnambulent realms of fantasy. Before long, however, both Onetti and his characters come to realize the futility of escape, and the confines of place and time become binding quagmires with which they have to cope. Thus, we see the elements of chronology and space as constant objects to be "defied" both by Onetti and his personages. This "defiance" has its basis in the realization that an escape from the clutches of these limitations is an impossibility. Both author and characters, therefore, in their own way, alternately resign themselves to indifference or attempt to reshape the inescapable destiny into something which is tolerable. We see, then, characters who invent their own geographical realms and who go so far as to impose their own inventions on their author, forcing him to accept them as part of his own imaginary horizon. We also see Onetti the author deliberately defying chronology in the sequence of his narrative and intentionally distorting the normal flow of events. These, however, are the consequences of Onetti's vision of time and place, of the elemental dimensions which define the boundaries of man's existence.

I A Fated Song of Innocence

Since Juan Carlos Onetti's first novel, El pozo (The Pit), is a key work, pivotal in the understanding of Onetti's oeuvre, the technical treatment of time and place in this work is also crucial for the sub-

54

sequent development of the author's novelistic craft. *El pozo,* by its intention (as stated by its protagonist), and for what he attempted to capture, could be called a "song of innocence." Once Onetti goes through the experience of this work he emerges, like his character, a changed man. Never again does he attempt in the same way to achieve those ends for which he tried in the first work, although one might say that Onetti's production in its entirety is an attempt at capturing what Linacero longed for in vain.

Onetti's first undertaking is a technical exercise in *delimitation.* To say that *El pozo* is not an expansive work would be an understatement; the objective of the author and the nature of his goal seem to be found, however, in the intentional lack of expansiveness. In what appears to be a deliberate exercise of delimitation, Onetti reduces the work to one character and the consciousness of that character, to the confines of one room, and to the breadth of one night, all symbolized by the title *(The Pit).* The objects of this exercise are primarily time and place. By reducing these to their minimum, the author seems to imply that what interests him is the immediate "here and now." This technical process points to an acute urgency in the author's pursuit. He seeks in the consciousness of his hero the resultant accretion of forty years as it exists at the moment and within the confines of that nocturnal cell in a boardinghouse.

In his attempt to capture the "here and now" Onetti is not unique. He represents a literary tradition ushered in by the twentieth century. Although the first Spanish American novelist with such a self-conscious objective, he has a kinship with writers such as Dorothy Richardson, Virginia Woolf, Proust, Joyce, and Faulkner. All of these writers, whose works predate Onetti, are preoccupied with the "here and now." They are considered the practitioners of the "psychological novel."[1] As such, the "here" becomes an extension of their own or their characters' consciousness; the "now" metamorphosizes itself from a chronological point in time to a psychic present whose boundaries become diffuse and whose beginning or end become imperceivable or insignificant.

Literary criticism tells us little about the end of the urgent pursuit of this immediacy. A study such as Leon Edel's *The Modern Psychological Novel* does not go beyond its excellent analytic exposition of technique. Technique, however, is merely a means. Nor does the available criticism of Juan Carlos Onetti's work attempt an explanation of what the writer seeks by using delimiting techniques which reduce space and time to an acute state of immediacy. In the case of novelists like Proust or Joyce, the writer himself becomes his own theoretician; their works include the process of their conception and making. We know, for example, that the "here and now" are the key to a lost childhood for Proust or, for Joyce, the arena of revelation of the quintessence of things through the epiphany. In the case of Onetti's first novel, however, we only know that Linacero, a man who decides to write his biography on the eve of his fortieth birthday, is attempting, as he tells us, to "pin the night like a butterfly" into an album. The endeavor proves futile. If we are then to take Onetti as reflecting himself and his art in his character, we only have a negative theory of literature, and specifically of his art. He may be saying, essentially, that whatever the artist seeks to achieve is unattainable, and he is therefore left with the "machinations" of the attempt as an end product. In this respect, though *Ulysses* and *El pozo* are very different works, they have a striking resemblance. What their authors give the reader in the end is merely the attempt, nothing more. Whether it is June 16, 1904, in Dublin or one anonymous night in a boardinghouse, in the end we are where we began. What we attain during the circular process (odyssey?) is dubious, perhaps a realization of an impossibility or a series of impossibilities.

The principal bearer or transmitting agent which carries the flow of Onetti's story is the night. Thus, the night, a measure and a denominator of time, bears Eladio Linacero's consciousness. This night, however, is manifold and refractory. It represents for one the time dimension of the narrative present; it reincarnates that distant night of twenty-five years ago when the event which triggers Linacero's memories takes place; it is also the oneiric night of fantasy, the night in which Linacero's dreams of "la cabaña de troncos" ("the log cabin") returns as a culmination to the night of the narrative present, when he finally stretches out in search of sleep and of the dream. Nonetheless, this multiple time dimension remains one and singular, just as Linacero's consciousness and its fragments of time converge into oneness, that is, into Linacero himself. This then is the "night" which Linacero seeks "to pin like a butterfly into a notebook." The confines, the geospatial boundaries of the "night" reappear in each of its multiple versions as a single room—a dark room, removed and solitary: the room of the gardener's house in the night of twenty-five-years ago when unintentionally, but instinctively, Linacero tried to violate Ana María; the room of the narrative present in the cheap boardinghouse; and the room of the evanescent "cabaña de troncos" in the distant Klondike mines and woods of Alaska.

Linacero, and Onetti through him, seem to be attempting to achieve a convergence, a merging of multiple time and space into a magical moment, an instant of illumined perception, in short, an epiphany, a point in time, arrested and out of time's ceaseless flow. This attempt on Onetti's part, oddly enough, *is* what it is by default. His pursuit, by his own admission, is not a Joycean epiphany nor a Proustian recapture and preserving of time, for Onetti's model is neither Joyce nor Proust; it is Faulkner.

Exactly ten years and two months before the publication of *El pozo*, Faulkner's *The Sound and the Fury* was published by Jonathan Cape and Harrison Smith. Like *El pozo*, it sat in the back rooms of bookshops and warehouses for a long time. In this work, Faulkner gives to the element of time an extratemporal quality. His technique consists of rendering time as neither chronological nor chronometric, but rather as a constantly unfolding past which holds the only reality in a character's life and consciousness. Again, this is not a chronological past, a point on the continuum of time; it is instead a totality in itself which contains both the present and the future. In short, it is the sum total of an individual's consciousness or, more accurately, the individual's consciousness is his past; thus the difference between Joyce and Faulkner and Proust and Faulkner. In *Ulysses*, for example, Stephen Dedalus lives the present through evoking the past, voluntarily or otherwise. Present situations call up past experiences which serve to expand and define the meaning of the present. Likewise, in Proust, the past is a distinct phenomenon to be reconstructed and relived Faulkner, on the other hand, " . . . does not laboriously reconstruct lost time in order to capture and preserve it as Proust does, trying to outwit it in a rational manner so typically French. Nor does he recreate time through an intense act of will as does Joyce, who enlarges intellectual consciousness and stretches it to its limit. Faulkner destroys time and throws it out of working order."[2]

Faulkner's characters therefore "do not rethink their past memories, they simply live them. . . . Christmas [in *Light in August*] lives his memories, whereas Proust relives them."[3] As such, "Christmas is not determined by his past [as is Dedalus]; he is his past."[4]

If we may take Linacero's confession as an indication of the
author's intention, Juan Carlos Onetti is, like Faulkner, attempting
to destroy time and its working order. Linacero tells us at the outset: "But now I would like to do something different. Something
better than the things which happened to me. I would like to write
the story of a soul, all by itself, without any of the events it had to
be involved in, whether it wanted to or not" (oc, 50 - 51). We see,
then, Linacero seeking a negation of the incidental. He is unlike
Dedalus who lives his present and depends upon past events at the
Clongowes Wood College of his childhood or the circumstances of
his mother's death, and unlike Marcel Proust whose consciousness
depends on the happenstance evocations of involuntary memory
and its circumstantial occurrences. This at least is his articulated
and conscious wish. Whether he succeeds to be unlike Dedalus or
Marcel is another question, which I shall return to shortly.
Nonetheless, the overt intentionality of Onetti's plan concurs with
the achievement of Faulkner. The negation of the circumstantial
and of the incidental in preference to the essential is an attempt at
destruction of those "successions" of time units, of the chronology,
in which these incidents happened to his hero. Although Linacero
denies "things that happened to me" ("las cosas que me
sucedieron") and "the events in which it had to envolve itself [the
soul]," ("los sucesos en que tuvo que mezclarse [el alma]") he still
wishes to write "the history of a soul" ("la historia de un alma").
What then is this history to include if not those things which this
soul had to experience? The question points very much to Faulkner.
Linacero seeks to become his past like Joe Christmas and the Comp-
sons, not a mere evocation or recollection of it. This reaching for the
distilled essence of the past is implicit in his words "the history of a
soul" ("historia de un alma"), for history implies a reality born of
the past. His pursuit then of the "here" and the "now" is for the
purpose of using these as a gateway into the essential self as constituted and derived from his past. The fact that his pursuit is an
overtly intentional and conscious attempt, however, necessarily implies the impossibility of its achievement which, in turn, signifies
Linacero's failure. Onetti seemingly attempts to give his character a
fateful destiny that emanates from within. He gives his hero, in addition, cognizance of this all-pervasive destiny, which means that
Linacero does not only live his fate but that he also has the power of
reflecting upon it. This reflection leads him inevitably to a desire for
understanding and implies a separation, a distance from that
destiny he attempts to become a part of and to comprehend.

Linacero is, undeniably, an intellectual hero. His creator conceived him as such and bestowed upon him an intellectual undertaking: "to write the history of a soul, of it alone" ("escribir la historia de un alma, de ella sola"). It is, therefore, his mental capacity which alienates Linacero from the very thing he tries to capture, the "here and now" ("la historia de un alma") and the past which comprises his total being. Thus, both Onetti and Linacero are representatives of the alienated modern intellectual who feels subject to an inescapable fate but who also possesses the power to perceive its futility and irremediability.[5] Neither Linacero nor Onetti succeeds in destroying chronological time; nor do they succeed in elevating the past to its Faulknerian ubiquity, for they are not capable of escaping objective reality and objective time. This is the purpose of the dream of "the log cabin." It occurs purely on the oneiric and psychological plane and therefore out of the realm of chronometric time. In Faulkner the psychological and purely subjective plane is where Benjy Compson's consciousness operates. He is an idiot and as such has a natural immunity to chronometry and objective reality, as does Joe Christmas who, like the majority of Faulknerian heroes, is far from being an intellectual. This absence of reflective power is perhaps why Faulkner's characters *are* their past and live it unquestioningly. We might call this an innate innocence. It is the innocence that Linacero sought, or at least sought to live and be, even for a moment, as if he were in possession of it.

Onetti's hero Linacero, however, is neither like Benjy nor like Christmas. He does not operate on one conscious plane but on three separate, temporal levels: the past, the narrative present, and the oneiric recurrence. For this reason he is aware, for example, that his subjective consciousness on the abstract plane is merely a dream. He is also conscious that his experience with Ana María of twenty-five years ago is merely a past. Benjy knows no difference, nor does Christmas, between the subjective and objective experiences. In addition, Linacero has cognizance of Onetti's narrative present. He cannot escape therefore from the objective "now." "But now I feel that my life is nothing more than the passing of fractions of time, one after another, one after another, like the sound of a clock, running water, a coin in counting. I am stretched out and the time passes" (*oc*, 75). Unable to destroy either objective chronology or objective reality, Linacero never attains a pure history of a soul, that is to say, an essential and pure past. What he does attain, and by default, is more of a Joycean epiphany which consists of the *quiditas* of his insurmountable inability to reach the state of innocence and blend entirely into his past. Thus, he admits: "I would have liked to pin the night on paper, like a nocturnal butterfly. But, in turn, it was the night that carried me off amid its waters; like the livid body of a dead man, it drags me inexorably in its cold and vagrant foam, down its night-stream" (*oc*, 76).

II   *A Song of Experience*

Two years after *El pozo*, in 1941, Onetti published *Tierra de nadie*. Both in technical, as well as in philosophical terms, the title of his second work attests to a maturation and a comprehension directly related to the first novel. Having lived through the vain attempt at innocence signified by Linacero's dream, Onetti now builds upon the lesson learned of the futility. Thus, *Tierra de nadie* represents a transition to the poetics of experience.

Criticism on Onetti unanimously places all of Onetti's works prior to *La vida breve*, which would include *El pozo*, *Tierra de nadie*, and *Para esta noche*, in one category. The two main reasons offered for this classification are first, that there is a lull of seven years between the last novel of this period and the appearance of *La vida breve* in 1950; second, that *La vida breve* introduces a new cycle based on the saga of Santa María which will dominate Onetti's subsequent works.

From a technical point of view, this classification seems somewhat arbitrary. In terms of technique one could say that *Tierra de nadie* has a greater affinity with *La vida breve* than with *El pozo*. In this respect, Onetti's first work should be considered in a special category, apart from any other; not because it is different from all other works of Onetti or any one work in particular, but because it has an equal affinity to all subsequent works of Onetti: it is this same quality of *El pozo* which makes it, in Emir Rodríguez-Monegal's terms, "a key novel" ("una novela clave") and is generally accepted as such by all critics. Whether the fecundity of *El pozo* was deliberate and conscious on Onetti's part we do not know, and it is immaterial. Perhaps we can only explain its importance in terms posited by the Argentine Jorge Luis Borges; that is, in so far as every writer creates his own precursors, works of art do the same.

We have seen in *El pozo* a deliberate effort to destroy objective reality and time, and failing that, an attempt at the evasion of this reality so noxious to the hero-confessor. We have also seen a complete failure to achieve these goals and therefore an inability on the character's part to attain a state of pure past, or pure being and essence outside of the ephemeral. Instead, he found himself within the grasp of this reality more than ever. The title of Onetti's second novel, *Tierra de nadie,* defines this experience on two levels; first, on the philosophical plane, which we might consider the author's vision of reality; the objective world which floats on chronological time is a no-man's-land. It cannot be captured, possessed, altered, or refined. Man and his consciousness are destined to constitute part of this inexorable flow with no particular end. Second, on a technical plane, the resignation and acceptance of the futility manifest at the end of the first novelistic experience led Onetti into a new attitude which will hereafter predominate in his craft.

Unable to overcome objective reality and the boundaries of time and place, Onetti confines his characters within these limitations. Thus, the overt intellectual confrontation with reality which Eladio Linacero was subjected to now becomes a natural and almost spontaneous state of being which sees the characters languishing with an attitude of acceptance, resignation, and outright indifference. To complete and accentuate this predicament, Onetti adapts a technique of simultaneity which blends the characters' consciousness with the experiences of the objective world. This consequently emanates a fragmentary and disjointed narrative which corresponds to the disconnected manner in which human consciousness experiences reality. Thus, objective time and place left to this natural propensity destroy themselves, for in real life there is no orderly sequence but rather a simultaneity with which human consciousness perceives the world. It is only language and the recounting of experience which is successive. In this respect, *Tierra de nadie* is more faithful to real life than *El pozo,* and, as such, represents a greater technical achievement on Onetti's part. We see, then, in this second work the unfolding of multiple dimensions, spatial as well as temporal, not through the microscope, as was the effect of *El pozo* and its confessional intimacy, but through a telescope, a cinematographic fish lens that is capable of bringing into the visual range all three hundred and sixty degrees. We also perceive an omniscience on the part of the narrator (Onetti), capable of projecting himself ubiquitously behind closed doors and into night streets simultaneously. This dimensional fragmentation extends also into the sphere of the narrative account, giving us a multiplicity of seemingly disconnected stories.

The technical practice of *delimitation* exercised in *El pozo* proves more natural in *Tierra de nadie* because, as a product of this fragmentation and simultaneity, it is a manifestation of the human capacity to perceive the objective world rather than an artifice of technique imposed upon the character. In the first page of *Tierra de nadie* we move with the narrator into at least three independent situations. The first is a static description of a taxi halting abruptly at a corner, jolting its passenger, a woman who perceives the fluorescent red of neon lights; the second is a scene inside a bedroom with a man sprawled in sleep, absent to the crimson-stained world touched by the red neon; the third is a fat man outside the bedroom, trying the door and finding it locked. James Irby calls the effect produced by these expressionistic and contrasting objects and perspectives "a mute testament of cinematography,"[6] adding that in this descriptive style of fragmenting objective reality we see a definite trace of Faulkner. The cinematographic effect to which Irby is referring, and on which Jaime Concha also elaborates, is found in the elements of transition which carry one scene into the next. The first scene, for example, is pervaded by the red of the neon whose "red strokes ran through the deserted flat roofs, fleetingly staining the sullen grey of the railings" ("golpes rojos se corrían por las azoteas desiertas, manchando fugazmente el gris hosco de los pretiles") (*oc*, 81). The perspective, as if through the lens of a camera, then moves from the rooftops and railings to the second situation. The verb with which the scene opens should be noted; it is a fluid verb denoting a plasticity in its action: "Running through the dirty window [the red neon stroke] reddened the smile of the man in the engraving fastened to the wall" ("Atravesando la ventana sucia, sonrojaban [los golpes rojos] la sonrisa del hombre en la lámina pegada a la pared"). Thus, the red-tinted eye of the camera has moved into the room in which "the hand of the sleeping man hung near the floor." The hand in the second scene introduces the third focus of our perspective which begins: "Outside, in the yellow light of the corridor, another hand advanced, closing on the latch. Locked. The fat man folded his fingers into a fist perturbed, and waited" ("Afuera, en la luz amarilla del corredor, otra mano avanzó, doblándose en el pestillo. Llave. El hombre gordo dobló los dedos fastidiado y esperó") (*oc*, 81 - 82). The carrier element which gives the thread of continuity is no longer the red stain of the light but the bulging hand of the sleeping man and the hand of the man outside the room ready to knock at the door. The tone of the narrative which flows from one scene and perspective to the next is one of cold indifference, completing the mechanical effect of a camera. This transitional element also gives the narrative descriptions an "expressionistic" quality.

It should be noted here that objective reality, unlike that of *El pozo*, is no longer an obsession, an inescapable trap. Its quality is still one of impurity, a stained and dirty entity; it does not, however, solicit the noxious response which it did in *El pozo*. Though this objective reality permeates the narrative, it is viewed with a mechanical indifference and not as an obsession. In this respect, Onetti is succeeding in the obliteration of this reality, reducing it to its fragmentary and circumstantial essence, and to its incidental representation of the human condition which it permeates. Jaime Concha, speaking of Buenos Aires as portrayed in *Tierra de nadie*, puts it this way: "Onetti reduces Buenos Aires to an insignificant, fragmentary mentioning, to street corners, to a skyscraper or other, to a reflection of a lit sign, to the intermittant presence of the river. . . . Fragmented into dispersed pieces, reduced to the vestiges of human situations, the Buenos Aires microtopography embodies the spiritual run of its inhabitants."[7]

The technical effect which Irby sees as a mute cinematographic testimony is not mere muteness but complete paralysis. What moves is not objective reality or chronology but the impersonal and mechanical seeing eye which produces the narrative description. The reality of the city and the time of the lives which move within its fragments are frozen to an immobile stillness. What Onetti's narrative furnishes is the history of this petrification. We see that the inexorably fluid "night" of *El pozo* has been halted, chronometrically and spatially, and therefore, the past is given free rein to permeate the stillness and to recount for us, as an old laminated photograph would do, that "story of a soul" which Linacero could not fully capture and which Onetti has now extended to a collectivity of stories. What we have, then, is a Faulknerian family or extended family whose histories give the cohesive thread to the fragments or "snapshots" of a barely pre - World War II Buenos Aires. In addition, we witness the frozen time and reality of which *The Sound and the Fury* is also constituted. Faulkner confines his work within three days, each holding the history of three

individuals which in unison form the history of a family and a society. Time and reality are frozen to such a point that Faulkner was
forced to supply an appendix to give the story some fluidity.
Analogously, *Tierra de nadie* offers us a series of congealed blocks,
fragments which pile up and whose sum forms a decipherable heap
of individual and collective pasts.

It is exactly through this stillness and petrification that Onetti
breaks chronological time and with which he destroys objective
reality. Time and reality are by nature dynamic; to have frozen
them implies their dissolution. This, in turn, implies that the
narrative's sole orientation is the past and what it contains. Thus,
the first human thought of *Tierra de nadie*, "We shall return
ourselves to each other like a ball, a reflection" ("Nos devolveremos
el uno al otro como una pelota, un reflejo . . .") (*oc*, 81), occurs to
the woman in the halting taxi of the opening scene. The past-
oriented nature of the thought is evident. The verb *devolveremos*
speaks more of what has been than of the impending encounter.
What we look to in the narrative is the meaning behind the anticipated act, that is, the meaning in the implied past. Since the second scene or fragment is static, the third presents another series of
implied pasts. We are introduced to an encounter between the man
at the door and the man who is sprawled inside, and to snatches of
circumstances which imply that there is a whole past history behind
this encounter whose unfolding we await. It is revealed piecemeal
through the involvement and implications of other circumstantial
"snapshots" which in turn imply other pasts. We have then the
collage, or montage, effect that we see in Faulkner. James Irby aptly points out the Faulknerian nature of Onetti's technique which is
comprised here of "offering only a fragment of the story and going
on revealing it little by little, interwoven with other fragments of
other stories."[8]

Within the isolated stillness of these fragments and frozen
histories there is one which speaks to us with an emblematic irony.
It is the fragment which opens up section eleven of the novel and
which deals with the taxidermist Pablo Num. The inclusion of this
episode and character in the novel represents the work's own
tautology. The episode is to *Tierra de nadie* what Edouard's journal
is to *Les Faux-Monneyeurs* and Stephen Dedalus' essay to *Portrait
of the Artist as a Young Man*. The three are tautological insofar as
they embody the central principle of the work in which they are in-

cluded. In a way, the episode is more than a tautology of this particular work. It is emblematic of all of Onetti's work and of the function of art in general.

Pablo Num is by profession a taxidermist. Thus, the object of his craft is petrification. He is blessed by a serene madness which drives him to create imaginary islands and to convince himself of the veracity of their existence. He stands in direct defiance to the process of chronology and spatial dynamics. A master at freezing time in stationary muteness, he is a reflection, a facsimile representation of his author-creator. The author, too, exercises a craft not unlike taxidermy to the point of even petrifying a river. The last scene of *Tierra de nadie*, for example, is no less a still statue than the animals in Pablo Num's shop: "Here he was sitting on the stone, with the last stain of the sea gull in the air and the stain of grease in the dirty, still, hardened river" ("Aquí estaba él sentado en la piedra, con la última mancha de la gaviota en el aire y la mancha de grasa en el río sucio, quieto, endurecido") (*oc*, 261).

Pablo Num's activity is not only reminiscent of Onetti's narrative descriptions, it also recalls some of the characters whom the author has taken out of the flow of time and movement in space. The earliest example occurs in Onetti's first work. Ana María of *El pozo* is and will always be eighteen years old in her statuesque form. Raquel of *La vida breve* will also always remain an adolescent. This, of course, brings to mind Faulkner's Benjy Compson, who at the chronological age of thirty-three is still three years old and will remain three perpetually. Faulkner, as well as Onetti, exercise a mastery in the art of embalming their characters. Thus, Jaime Concha's observation with respect to Onetti's characters that "Each being is a mummy of its own past"[9] goes beyond the implication that we find the meaning of each character's life in their past; it is also an accurate statement of actuality in some cases.

Taxidermy is not particularly alien to the function of art in general. Certain artists have placed their hopes entirely in this process. For writers like Proust who find their only salvation in art, art is a conserver in the face of time's destructive course; it preserves life or beauty in spite of the passing of time and the changes it precipitates. In this respect, art also embalms, petrifies, and sustains a form out of time.

The Pablo Num episode is also significant for another reason. His contagious obsession with the imaginary never-never-land of

Faruru, which was to infect Onetti irrevocably, resulted in the do-
main of the mythical Santa María around which we witness the
founding of an entire saga.

Para esta noche (1943), Onetti's third novel, is an elaboration of
the novelistic technique that the author achieves with his second
work, *Tierra de nadie,* two years earlier. Its spatial and time dimensions are the same. Buenos Aires once again supplies the arena. Its
nocturnal streets and buildings, the isolated rooms in which the
characters, who are emanations of mysterious pasts, languish. This
work is of more importance to my following chapter on narrative
point of view, and I shall therefore put off till then discussion of its
technical makeup. It is the first novel in which not only does
geographical and chronological fragmentation take place, but there
is also a bifurcation of the narrative thread more akin to Faulkner's
Sartoris and to the final part of *The Sound and the Fury.*

Before moving on to Onetti's second phase (opening with *La
Vida breve*) in which time and space acquire mythical and legendary dimensions, I should like to say something concerning the implicit metaphysics which underlie the technical recourses of the first
three novels. One may speculate that it is this metaphysics which
made resorting to a mythical plane necessary. The author's vision of
reality, his experience with the elemental dimensions of time and
space, might have forced him into seeking an alternative reality
which would be more manageable or, perhaps, a reality which by
mere fact that it has its origin in the author and his work would be
less deterministic and less pervasively dominating. A brief focus on
the author's metaphysics of time and space might throw some light
on these speculations.

The metaphysics of Juan Carlos Onetti is the metaphysics of time
and space, the defining limits which circumscribe the human condition. "Man's misfortune," says Sartre, speaking of William
Faulkner, "lies in his being time-bound."[10] Onettian man is not
only time-bound, he is also fated to dawdle and languish, hemmed
in by an inescapable geography. "Misfortune" is too generous an
adjective for him, for it implies something noble, like the enduring
augustness which one associates with tragedy. We have none of
these connotations in Onetti's world until perhaps in the last events
of the saga of Santa María, related in *El astillero.* What we have instead is a pervasive pathos which emanates an indifferent acceptance. It is this difference between Onetti and Faulkner that leads
Luis Harss to conclude, "Faulkner is a tragedian; Onetti, if one can
coin a term, is a pathetician."[11]

The instances in which there is any will to action on the part of Onetti's heroes are indeed scarce. One can actually count the instances and discover that the nature of these actions point to Onetti's vision of time and place vis-à-vis his characters. Such an enumeration would readily establish two categories. In the first we see characters like Llarvi of *Tierra de nadie* and the unnamed basketball player of *Los adioses* whose will to action is suicidal.[12] To the second category belong characters like Eladio Linacero of *El pozo*, Juan María Brausen of *La vida breve*, and Junta Larsen in collusion with Petrus of *El astillero*. The will to action is directed in pursuit of an alternate reality set in the realm of fantasy, the abstract, and the imaginary. Both categories, one readily notices, are rooted in evasion, in attempts to elude and even to prevaricate, if not to consummately abdicate the human condition and reality to which these characters are subject. This consistent attitude on the part of his "heroes" epitomizes Onetti's vision of man, together with the time and the geographical confines to which human nature is fated. Thus, beginning with *El pozo* we see in Eladio Linacero a negation of time and circumstance, and an attempt on the part of the character to regain a state transcendental to chronology and physical reality.

The effort, as we have seen, proved to be useless. *Tierra de nadie* and *Para esta noche* incorporate this futility and emanate a negative metaphysics of time and place, which manifests itself in the stagnancy of chronometry, allowing a more fundamental time to reign, one more powerful than the clocks and dates that man invented for himself. This negativity becomes flagrant in the fragments of a murky cosmos. On both planes, physical and temporal, the world of these novels is under siege: in *Tierra de nadie* a metaphysical, symbolic siege by an unleashed past and a fateful accretion of fragments of time and events; in *Para esta noche*, we have a metaphysical siege plus a literal one by which the characters find themselves under a military curfew.

La vida breve, Onetti's fourth novel, which opens up a new phase in the author's career, is a synthesis. Metaphysically, it reconciles *El pozo*'s direct attack on objective reality with the futile or negative metaphysics which underlie *Tierra de nadie* and *Para esta noche*. What this synthesis produces and its subsequent fate is the focus of the following section of this chapter.

III   *Transmigration to the Mythical*

In his psychoanalytic study of William Faulkner's *Sanctuary*, the psychiatrist Lawrence S. Kubie observes that: "When a man feels unable to achieve some goal toward which he is struggling, he can in his fantasy handle his sense of powerlessness in one of several ways. In the first place, he can people the whole world with other impotent figures, spreading his own infirmity to include everyone, and thus reducing his feeling of painful humiliation."[13] The work of Juan Carlos Onetti is populated with figures that manifest an overwhelming feeling of impotence and helplessness in the face of objective reality. These characters are bound and trapped in a quagmire which progressively engulfs them. In Onetti's first phase, this quagmire takes on a labyrinthine circular quality. For example, we see Linacero at the end of *El Pozo* back where he was at the opening passage of the novel. In *Tierra de nadie*, the final passages, Chapters 60 and 61, bring us back to the inhumanly mute atmosphere with which the novel began, including the flashing red of the neon lights. The work ends with a petrification in which everything is behind the man, Aránzuru, who stands staring at the still river with his back to the city. He has witnessed a chapter of this metropolis' chronicles as captured by the novel; and the city goes on as it always has and always will, unchanged, with no end: "It was already night and the city buzzed under the lights, with its men, its hats, children, handkerchiefs, shopwindows, steps like blood, like hail, steps like a current without a destination" (*oc*, 261). Onetti brings us back to where we started, with a summation of where we have hopelessly been. Similarly, *Para esta noche* ends under the same siege with which it began: military terror still steadfastly chokes the city with its ruthless grasp.

The works in their circularity become metaphysical tautologies of themselves. Time takes on the dimensions of an endlessly unfolding circle with an omnipresent center which is the ominous past. Geographically, the progress of these novels is nil except for a symbolic advance which is rather a descent into greater depths of powerlessness and resignation. If anything, in terms of linear geographical progression, there is a closing in of the environment like the motion of a snail's configuration. The movement reaches a point of isolation at the putative tip of its circular structure. We get this feeling in the third to last paragraph of *Tierra de nadie:* "There was no longer an island to sleep on in the entire old earth, nor friends, nor women for company" (*oc*, 261). Progression, therefore, chronological as well as geographical, has only served to individuate and isolate man to the ultimate extreme.

Having reached this forlorn point on the shell of the snail, Onetti's narrative world takes the only recourse possible. It jumps from the spatial and chronological dimension into a second degree imaginary zone, into a twilight zone of fantasy and myth. It is a "new" narrative trajectory that eventually will prove to be, in terms of dynamic time and space, another snail shell, a circular labyrinth to the second degree. With this jump, Onetti confirms Kubie's observation cited above. If hitherto the novelistic world of Onetti was merely a manifestation of a metaphysics, after *La vida breve* and Juan María Brausen it becomes a world in the image of Onetti's helplessness. His characters from now on will be accurate mirror images of himself in the struggle to create alternate and imaginary worlds not unlike those of the author. Onetti will even accept the psychotic and schizoid creation of Juan María Brausen and offer him refuge in this realm at the end of *La vida breve*, thus transforming the fantasy world into a "concrete phenomenon" which will eventually assume mythical and legendary proportions. We could say, therefore, that all of Onetti's work subsequent to *La vida breve* is an emanation of Juan María Brausen's psychotic mind. It is as if Onetti accompanied Brausen into an insane asylum and viewed through a microscope the contents of Brausen's fantasy. In this way those pathetic destinies accumulated in the first phase of Onetti's work transmigrate—as their progress proves—without any change into the mythical world of Santa María which was born of Brausen's psychosis.

This jump to a second degree fictional plane gives Juan Carlos Onetti an indirect approach to the problem of time and space, both in technical as well as philosophical terms. He now is operating within a space-time medium twice removed from his daily life and the life of the reader. This could be considered an abdication of the objective world on the part of the author himself, much like that of his protagonists who find refuge in their fantasies. There seems to have been no other alternative open, however. By the end of this first period, Onetti spiraled into a dead end, technically as well as metaphysically. This jump, therefore, should be viewed as a resumption of the process of solving the problem of fiction and of reaching for an existential solution to man's query on a different plane. By removing the problem to a second level, Onetti now has put a distance between his existential dilemma and the dilemma of man on a broader, universal scale, one more step removed from the situation of the reader as well. The virtue of the tactic lies clearly in

the objectivity which the perspective of distance offers. When Emir
Rodríguez-Monegal considers, though he does not elaborate, in his
prologue to Onetti's *Obras completas*, Juan María Brausen as
"legitimate descendent of Linacero" (*oc*, 21), he is speaking of
Onetti's problem as a writer. The implication, in my view, is that
the problem remains the same but seen in a new light, with a
renewed approach to its solution. This new light attests to an evolution and further maturation on the part of Onetti as a writer. The
change is similar to the one of which Karsten Harries speaks:

> The very attempt to reveal a reality which man's individual understan-
> ding hides from him, seems contradictory. What is revealed must always re-
> main at a distance; the ideal of an existence not rent by the polarities of
> consciousness can be posited but not realized. *Innocence is not recaptured
> by direct attack.* But if the direct route seems impossible, may it not be
> possible to try a more indirect approach? Instead of trying to reach for that
> which lies behind the veil of the finite, the artist can try to lift or tear this
> veil. Such art would once more be negative; yet at the same time it would
> strive for revelation. It would negate only to remove those obstacles that
> prevent man from escaping from the finite spirit and its world and thus
> return him to the origin.[14]

The passage indicates clearly the road traversed by Onetti from *El
pozo* to *La vida breve* and in a way sums up my discussion to this
point. It also points to another problem in Onetti with regard to the
fate of the alternate and indirect approach through myth which the
author has taken.

The question under consideration is, What happens to Onetti's
approach through myth? Before exploring this topic further, I
should like to elaborate on the origin of the mythical plane to which
Onetti has transposed his aesthetic battleground. The process of this
origin offers a tautology of Onetti's own evolution within the
broader scope of his career.

I spoke above (at the end of the last section in this chapter) of *La
vida breve* as representing a synthesis in Onetti's literary world.
This novel manages to reconcile concurrently two extremes on a
technical as well as on a metaphysical plane. We see once again a
return to the first work, *El pozo*, as well as an elaboration of the two
subsequent novels.

La vida breve begins on a note all too familiar for anyone who is
acquainted with *El pozo*. The work opens with the narrative of a
confessor-narrator. The setting of time and place is also familiar; as

in *El pozo* and *Tierra de nadie,* it is the night in a room of a city apartment, four walls and a nocturnal symphony that emanates from the dissonant consciousness of the hero-confessor. Time and its flow are purely subjective and psychological. The coercive propellants of chronology are beyond the narrator's control. He gets his cues, as does the reader, from external occurrences. These markers and determinants of time's passing are spatially removed yet claustrophobically dominating. The first of these elements is Juan María Brausen's obsessive memory of his wife's scarred body; it is a memory and therefore uncontrollable, since it is separated from him by time and place. The second motif which marks off the passing of time consists of the events in the adjacent apartment. These events dominate and control his sense of chronology and yet remain separated literally by a wall and consequently out of his reach.

The metaphysics of negativity rampant in *Tierra de nadie* and *Para esta noche* also prevail here. Time and place serve to individuate, isolate, and alienate. Whereas the futile dynamics of space dominated *Tierra de nadie* as the title attests, in *La vida breve* the controlling element is time; again the title is more than symbolic. Juan María Brausen is made aware of the futility which pervades Onetti's second work. He languishes like Aránzuru and his cohorts. He does not resign himself to their indifference, however, nor does he abdicate life through suicide as Llarvi did. With this cognizance of fatal negativity he sets out to pursue, like Eladio Linacero, an alternative, not necessarily the innocence that Linacero was after. Brausen appears as a reincarnation of Eladio Linacero but with the significant advantage of having dreamed and thus having become wise: "I awoke talking; I saw my stupidity, my impotence, my lie occupy the place of my body and take its form" ("Me recordé hablando; vi mi estupidez, mi impotencia, mi mentira ocupar el lugar de mi cuerpo y tomar su forma") (*oc,* 442). Brausen's affirmation is a song of experience. Nevertheless, his pursuit is similar to Linacero's attempts of ten years earlier. As in the latter's case, corporeality, that is to say, objective reality as it functions in concrete time and space, is denied: here it dissolves; in *El pozo* it proved invincible. Salvation in both cases, however, is sought in parallel fashion. What is significant is the divergent planes on which its realization is sought. Juan María Brausen is conscious of his impotence; he feels the stupidity of reaching for the unattainable ideal, and the lie promised by man's capacity to dream. It is with the consciousness of these vain hopes that he seeks to construct his salvation. This salvation will consist precisely of the impotence and lie of which man is made. As Brausen tells us early in the novel: "I convinced myself that I alone was ready to save myself from that night which was beginning just beyond the balcony, exciting, with its diffuse gusts of warm wind. I kept my head bent over the light on the desk; at times I threw it backward and looked at the reflection of the lampshade on the ceiling, an incomprehensible shape that promised a rectangular rose. Beneath my hands I had the paper for my salvation, a blotter and the fountainpen" (*oc*, 455 - 56). Brausen's intent, however, is far from capturing "the history of a soul." He knows better than to expect an ideal state of purity and innocence. What he seeks to engender on the blank paper which faces him is another human being, an incarnation of impotence, futility, and resignation. He is to be called Dr. Díaz Grey and is to represent a world, that of Santa María, also an invention of Brausen's attempt at self-salvation. Brausen's first description of this man is revealing: "There is an old man, a doctor that sells morphine. Everything has to begin from there, from him. Perhaps he is not old; but he is tired, dried up" ("Hay un viejo, un médico, que vende morfina. Todo tiene que partir de ahí, de él. Tal vez no sea viejo, pero está cansado, seco") (*oc*, 441). What immediately comes to mind is Lawrence Kubie's observation with respect to Faulkner's *Sanctuary* cited at the beginning of this section. Onetti's world seems to be populated with futility and impotence and reproduces itself with ironic fecundity.

As for Onetti, the creator and mastermind of these ectoplasmic worlds, Brausen and *La vida breve* represent a new and indirect attack on the thought of recapturing whatever it is that gives man a grasp of life's essence, an understanding whose acquisition engenders peace or at least bearable acceptance of the human condition. From what Brausen sets out to do we see that there is still a desire for salvation; from the manner in which he sets out, we gather that the negative vision and metaphysics hitherto pervading still continue to occupy a primary role. The fact that this undertaking is reconciled and put under the auspices of such a metaphysics with a continuous persistence in its fervor, is a clear indication that *La vida breve* represents a moment of synthesis, a summation and resolution, in Onetti's career. I think it is of crucial significance that Brausen insists on one particular trait his creation must have: "This doctor ought to have had a past that would

perhaps be decisive and explicatory, that would not interest me"
(*oc*, 442). Brausen's insistence that Díaz Grey have a decisive and
explicatory past is a clear reflection of Onetti's vision of time; his affirmation that this past should be of no interest to him is an indication of Onetti's metaphysics of time as it has evolved since *El pozo*.

As early as the short stories of the early 1930s, we see Onetti's
hero not particularly interested in the past as a repository of man's
life but rather as a culmination which floods the present and reveals
or explains to him what the present is. In *Tierra de nadie* and *Para
esta noche*, as already pointed out, the past is all-pervasive. What
we have are snatches of petrified lives illumined by the past. *La
vida breve* takes this fragmentation of lives, which are already past
as they are narrated, and strings them together to reveal and unfold
a human history. As the work's title indicates, Onetti offers us a
series of "short lives" lived by various characters or simply by one
character, as is the case of Juan María Brausen-Arce-Díaz Grey, all
within the psyche of one character. As a result of this process one
can say that Onetti is transforming time into space. All these
fragments, these short lives, strung together form a kind of a mural
which we could follow visually in its static display.

Just as Brausen expresses no interest in the past of Díaz Grey (for
if he did he would end up confronting himself and his human condition face to face again) Onetti elaborates on little or none of the
past of Brausen, except as it unfolds in the present with its schizoid
multiplicity. This multiplicity is what gives Onetti's *La vida breve*
three-dimensional character, that is to say, dynamism, and elevates
it from a flat unidimensional "biography," as was the case to some
extent with *El pozo*. Díaz Grey and Santa María then are another
time-space dimension. The pretext of the invention further attests
to this process of transforming the temporal to the spatial. Brausen
after all conceived the provincial doctor and his environment as a
cinematographic script. There is no more obvious process of
transforming time into space than the cinema, a genre which is
capable of altering lifetimes and centuries of chronology into a
spatial plane perceivable by the human consciousness in a matter of
an hour or more. Once again, however, this spatial plane that has
absorbed chronometry and its flow is not left as a unilateral or unidimensional phenomenon. It is given depth, dynamism, and a
refractory character by the author. The world of Santa María
becomes, as I already mentioned, the refuge of the fugitive Arce-
Brausen at the end of *La vida breve*. Furthermore, nine years later,

Para una tumba sin nombre, Onetti's sixth novel, is narrated by
Díaz Grey and occurs in Santa María. Hereafter, Santa María
becomes the arena of Onetti's fiction and Díaz Grey an old-time
denizen who has absorbed and can reveal much of the realm's
history. Santa María then takes on mythical proportions. Onetti's
narrative world becomes an elaboration of the men and annals of
the city of Santa María, and from it spring such masterpieces as *El
astillero* and *Juntacadáveres.*

In this mythical realm of a poetic geography time stands still, and
becoming yields to being. The only dynamism that chronology and
time have left is in the succession of narration, but once narrated,
once recounted, becoming ceases again and becomes petrified.
What ensues is a timelessness which algebraically and reciprocally
negates even space. The result of this is a work like *El astillero*
(1961) whose antagonist is Petrus. The role of time in the story comes to light as an apposition to Junta Larsen's relentlessness to give
into its deconsecration, thus bringing about his own self-destruction
and nullification. Space is also abrogated, for it has the same
stillness and decadence as time, both symbolized by the antagonist,
his name, and his madness. For madness, too, is a mechanism of
timelessness, as we already have observed in Faulkner's Benjy
Compson.

Onetti's *El astillero* is a culmination of the author's program and
his new trajectory which originates with *La vida breve* and the
founding of Santa María. It represents both a technical as well as a
metaphysical apex. It is a crystallization of Onetti's narrative structure as well as of his expression. Applying Karsten Harries' assertion
cited above, *El astillero* is a return to the origin, the author's
original vision of reality and the human condition through an "indirect approach" and "negative art."

The ebbing into which Onetti spiraled just prior to *La vida breve*
once again looms large over the author and his narrative world. *El
astillero* represents an even larger circumnavigation which returns
to *El pozo* and Eladio Linacero. Although the progressive
gradations of unreality have multiplied and reproduced themselves,
in the end the sole recourse open to the inhabitants of the Onettian
cosmos is self-deception. Linacero resorts to the phantasmagory of a
dream; the dwellers of *El astillero* to empty gesticulations, to in-
consequential ritual motions around the carcass of a wharf and
shipyard long rendered defunct and useless by erosive time. The
path traversed has seen the Onettian heroes move from fiction, to
escapist fantasy, to myth, and back to bizarre self-delusion.

The circularity of the narrative, by now a saga, is evident with the opening paragraph of *El astillero*. What we witness there is a return, the return of the protagonist, Junta Larsen, to the Santa María he was forced to abandon five years earlier. The circumstances of Larsen's departure and the events which perpetrated it are revealed to us in *Juntacadáveres* (1964), which appears after *El astillero* but whose partial composition precedes it.

Defeated and pessimistic, Junta Larsen returns to the past *(El astillero)*. Having found no redeeming significance of lasting quality in his abortive ventures, he reverts to the bygone for some sort of salvation and meaning. Oddly enough, this past is the very same one which vanquished his hopes of an earlier epoch. Having gone this far into the paradoxical paradigm, it is not surprising that Larsen should undertake the task, futile from the beginning, of resuscitating a musty and rusted derelict shipyard and seek through this undertaking the self-redemption and affirmation he was never able to attain. The very idea of the undertaking is a defiance, an arrogant and desperate challenge to time, since it is attempted within the very heart of its destructive emanations.

To the extent that in Onetti's narrative time and spatial dynamics are cyclical, it is quite natural to return to the past. It is really not a return but an inevitable arrival at a point on the circumference already traversed. This inevitability engenders and points to another. The other inescapable certainty is the nature of the human condition; for little changes in the motion of a circle or series of circles. The direction of the revolutions remains the same and so does their velocity. To attempt a new direction or to reject the pace implies a necessary falling into the void. This finality is precisely that of Junta Larsen. Utterly pessimistic as it may seem, death is the only salvation for the Onettian hero. In *El astillero* this fate seems to be the wrath of time, a merciless reply to Larsen's defiance.

El astillero could be viewed as an arena for redemption and perdition; an arena in which time enjoys complete sovereignty and is capable of leveling off any serious obstacle which might present itself. Junta Larsen occupies such a position and represents one of three gradations in the novel with respect to time. He plunges earnestly into the task of resuscitating that which time has destroyed. Larsen is the only one who undertakes this task with sincerity and resolution. In direct opposition to Larsen is the high priest of this graveyard, Petrus. He, too, is sincere, but his sincerity is not an emanation of reflective intent; rather, it is a blessing of madness which convinces him successfully of the validity of his game at make-believe. His dementedness is all-pervasive and infectious. What proceeds from him is similarly infected, his daughter being the most glaring specimen.

Between Larsen and Petrus stand the two "functionaries," Kunz and Gálvez, and the latter's wife. The first two are just what their title implies, functionaries that unquestioningly perform their ritualistic motions, empty as they might be. They have given in to the game either because they are not willing or because they are not capable of anything else; most likely it is the latter. They persist at humoring Petrus and subsist by junking and selling the useless parts of the shipyard. In this respect they are as much agents of corrosive time as Petrus. The woman, bulging with pregnancy, is a symbol of natural and instinctual life. She is Onetti's version of Faulkner's Lena Grove (in *Light in August*). Her existence is crowned by that timeless perseverance and tenacity—timeless because she is unquestioning of time and even unconscious of its passing, an unawareness indicated by the surprise with which labor takes her, and by her unquestioning giving in to the bearing of a new life. She will in the end be the true counterpart to Junta Larsen and his despair.

Larsen's steadfast intentness, in the face of these resigned attitudes, accentuates the desperate character which his attempts at redemption have taken. For him, the shipyard and its revival represent a last chance. The others have nothing to save. The game for them has taken on a normalcy; its fiction has become their reality. Thus, they have nothing but the game. For Larsen the play is a means to and from which he must transcend. This transcendence, of course, must also defy time. In a moment of illumined realization, however, Larsen becomes aware of the impossibility of his last attempt, and in the face of its hopelessness rejects the irredeemable. He rejects life. Thus, he runs with terror and disgust from the sanguine scene of the woman's child bearing. He also repudiates his own life, giving himself up to death. He abandons precisely that which he sought to redeem. In the face of time, then, nothing human is redeemable, neither the work of man, symbolized by the shipyard, nor his life.

Some twenty years earlier Eladio Linacero came to the same conclusion. At the end of *El pozo* he gives himself up to the inexorable flow of time and its night. Then, it was on a realistic plane within the mirror image of life's context. Now, it is on the mythical level, woven intricately enough by the author to prove as faithful to reality as life itself. Consequently, the end is the same. For in the metaphysics of Onetti and his vision of the human reality, man carries his condition with him, regardless of the dimensional plane on which his destiny unfolds. "The past," says Borges, "is indestructible; sooner or later all things will return, including the plan to abolish the past."

CHAPTER 4

"Through the Looking Glass":
Narrative Point of View

I Perspectives

IN terms of a writer's craftmanship or technique, point
of view is, above all, the author's relationship to his narrative.
Whether a writer relates his story to us directly, whether he chooses
a spokesman or assigns the task to one of the story's personages, or
whether he makes himself invisible altogether and allows his story
to "tell itself," his presence as the mastermind of what we behold
can never be forgotten altogether. Even when reading an
anonymous work, the reader is wont to conjure some image of a
creator behind it. By the nature of his craft, therefore, the writer is
compelled to cope with the problem of where to place himself in
relation to his world and in what manner. The problem is crucial,
for upon it frequently hinges the success or failure of his work.

Furthermore, point of view is the relationship of the narrator to
the story, to the author (if he is distinctly separate), to the reader,
and to the other characters (if any) in the story. There is in the
reading of any work an implicit dialogue between author, narrator,
other characters, the reader, and resultant interrelationships among
all of these. The term "point of view" encompasses all such
relationships from the perspective of an aesthetic distance, which
may be moral and/or physical.[1]

Narrative point of view has been one of the most crucial problems
for twentieth-century literature as indicated by contemporary
criticism's constant preoccupation with this problem. Onetti as a
novelist of this century has had to confront this problem and has
done so in a manner crucial to Spanish American fiction. Thus, a
few general comments on point of view I believe are necessary and
germane.

78

With the advent of writers like Henry James, literary criticism seems to agree that a new epoch in storytelling has dawned. The writer has become self-conscious of his role as writer in society and as author of his work. The new horizons opened up in the field of psychology, as Leon Edel points out,[2] have presented the writer with novel recourses, as well as posed new queries in narrating. With the rise of individualism, a new image of man and therefore new expectations in literary heroes and narrators have been introduced. This individualism coupled with the new psychology eventually individuates contemporary man to the point of exasperating alienation and thus gives rise to a new philosophy of man in his existential circumstance. Turned in upon himself, modern man is frustrated by the disparity in the ideals and demands he finds within and the contrasting actualities he has to face from without. In the twentieth century, it is alleged, the individual finds that he is to confront his human situation without many precedents from the past. Undoubtedly, this new circumstance leads to a self-image that engenders an analogously novel concept of literary man and of man within literature. Literature, as an emanation of man's life and struggle for survival, of his victories and failures toward this goal, thus necessarily undergoes the same changes, and this includes, of course, the manner of relating or of recounting literature, or the point of view through which literature is presented to the reader.

All this concerns the philosophical plane on which narrative point of view unfolds, rather than the technical one. In a writer's predilections with regard to point of view we can discern his vision of art and of man in the general task of creativity. The author's metaphysics and view of literature are often implied in his vision. And, since in the final analysis an author writes in order to communicate, his particular narrative point or points of view include his position on the possibility of human communication and communion among men. Finally, all this undoubtedly does reveal an author's view of himself, as artist and as man. Thus, it is not very difficult to appreciate the obsessive preoccupation of writers and critics with the manner and means by which a story is to be related to the reader.

The twentieth century is also a godless age. The idea of a mastermind conceiving the cosmos and revealing it to us, making his omnipotence constantly felt in the process, is outmoded. The mere idea of such a phenomenon is at best relegated to a thematic undercurrent in modern literature. Analogously, the modern reader and literary critic often repudiate the self-deification of any writer within his work. The tendency, then, is for the author to disappear, to make himself invisible and allow his cosmos to reveal itself. One of the most articulate readers and critics to voice this demand is Percy Lubbock: "The art of fiction does not begin until the novelist thinks of his story as a matter to be shown, to be so exhibited that it will tell itself."[3]

Writing in 1939 on François Mauriac's *La Fin de la nuit*, Jean Paul Sartre demonstrates accurately and succinctly the modern reader's expectations of a novel and of a novelist and, in a way, sheds light on our century's concept of literature. He begins his essay by saying: "The novel does not present things, but rather their signs."[4] We are automatically reminded of the phantasmal nature of a writer's labors. Literature, therefore, pertains to the realm of "signs" and its creators are subject to this realm. Their overt imposition on "things," on reality, ours, the reader's, has no place in their task. Sartre concludes: "M. Mauriac has put himself first. He has chosen divine omniscience and omnipotence. But novels are written *by* men and *for* man. In the eyes of God, who cuts through appearances and goes beyond them, there is no novel, no art, for art thrives on appearances. God is not an artist. Neither is M. Mauriac."[5]

II   El pozo

In that same year of 1939, *El pozo*, a scant ninety-nine-page novel, on what looks like shopping-bag paper, appeared in Montevideo. It is doubtful that Onetti had read Sartre's work prior to the writing of his novel. Yet, the manner in which the story unfolds follows the precepts of literature and art articulated by Sartre in his essay on Mauriac. For critics like Emir Rodríguez-Monegal and writers like the Peruvian Mario Vargas Llosa, *El pozo* marks the birth of a new era, the rise of the creative and contemporary novel in Latin America. Mario Vargas Llosa writes, "It would be more correct to date the birth of the Latin American novel to 1939, with the appearance of *El pozo*, the first novel by the Uruguayan novelist Juan Carlos Onetti."

The Peruvian author continues, explaining his assertion by pointing out Onetti's unique achievement as a Latin American writer:

Onetti is perhaps chronologically the first novelist of Latin America who, in a series of works . . . has created a world both scrupulous and coherent, which is important in itself and not for the informative material it contains, and which is accessible in any language to readers anywhere, because the subject matter has acquired, by virtue of a "functional" language and technique a universal dimension. It is no longer an artificial world we are presented with, but a world that is human before it is American and one which, like all creations of a lasting nature, consists in the objectivization of something subjective, where the primitive novel had constituted the subjectivization of a selected objective reality.[6]

Point of view is part of that technique that Vargas Llosa describes as having given Onetti's work "a universal dimension" and is the primary agent in the "objectivization of something subjective." *El pozo*, which commences Onetti's project toward this end is structured in such a way that the author can "disappear," and the subjective world of his story and of his hero-narrator can objectify itself for the reader. The work's center of reference is the consciousness of Eladio Linacero and his sphere of experience. This is precisely what the reader beholds unfolding itself before his eyes. Onetti, the author, has become invisible by integrating himself into his character-narrator so convincingly that we do not feel his presence or omniscience. There is only one registering consciousness within the work, and what comes across to us is its record through a narrative process that Sartre would call "unmediated realism." *El pozo* is unquestionably a subjective novel. The first-person narration which binds the reader to the senses and experience of the hero-narrator is precisely the mode of this genre. As Leon Edel points out in his chapter on "A Logic of Subjectivity," "The author's purpose in the subjective novel is to place the reader within the consciousness of a character."[7]

The narrative time within this manner of "recounting" is inevitably the present of the narrator's experience. The story is no longer that which occurred "once upon a time," rather it unfolds in the psychological time of now. By the fact that time is psychological and not chronological, lapses or references to other temporal dimensions are not excluded. This is precisely what occurs in *El pozo* as well as in later works of the author.

Although Henry James seems to be accepted by modern criticism as the technical father of the contemporary novel, Eladio Linacero is a far cry from that Jamesian "central intelligence" which il-

luminates the narrative and which is indispensable to any good
novelist. However, Onetti never claimed to have understood James,
but he has confessed his affinity with Faulkner who, in Rodríguez-
Monegal's terms, "directly or indirectly, has attended the school of
James."[8] For that matter, Benjy Compson in his idiocy is inadequate as a narrator and even farther removed from that "central intelligence." We should keep in mind, however, that *The Sound and
the Fury* is a four-part novel that like Lawrence Durrell's *Alexandria Quartet* mirrors itself among its various parts and gives some
comprehensible explications in these interreflected mirror images.
The last part of Faulkner's novel, the Dilsey segment, is even
narrated by such a "central intelligence" as is Durrell's *Mountolive*
in the heart of the *Quartet*. This mirroring in which a work reflects
upon itself an explication is a recourse which Onetti successfully
adapts as early as his second novel, *Tierra de nadie* and which he
elaborates, as Vargas Llosa states, into a self-sufficient and comprehensible cosmos beginning with *La vida breve*.

An aesthetic, and therefore philosophical, explanation is at the
heart of *El pozo's* technique in narrative point of view. This brings
us back to Sartre's reservations about François Mauriac. It is also
reminiscent of Albert Camus' *La Peste;* and we should keep in mind
the thematic crux of Camus' work, namely; that no man's circumstance can truly be told or related to another man and that no
man can speak for another, since he is not that man nor his existential circumstances. We should also remember that both *La Nausée*
and *L'Etranger* have equally "inadequate" first-person narrators
with as great a self-consciousness of what they are doing within the
novel as has Eladio Linacero.

The world which Onetti puts before us demands both the
narrative technique and the narrator that he utilizes. It is a matter
of congruity between form and content, and also an internal consistency that Linacero the narrator should be conscious of his act of
narration for he, as a type, is a function of the theme and story
which he is narrating. His locus or point of view is also a
philosophical locus, and for the explanation of this I turn to
Kierkegaard and Karsten Harries. The latter, in his chapter on "The
Aesthetics of Subjectivity," sums up what I am attempting to say
about Onetti as follows: "In the first volume of *Either/Or*
Kierkegaard describes such a romantic nihilist. His aesthete no
longer tries to draw away the veil hiding the infinite; he does not
believe in a saving beyond in even this weak and rather foggy sense.

He finds himself alone and bored in a world which is indifferent to his demand for meaning. Yet the demand for meaning persists. Despairing of discovering meaning, he attempts to invent it and thus to escape from the absurdity of his situation."[9]

This passage describes Onetti as accurately as it describes Eladio Linacero, and the undertaking of a work like *El pozo* is an attempt on two levels which, through the adequate use of point of view, mirror each other. Onetti seems to hold the Kierkegaardian position and seems to know that it is also descriptive of himself. Through the use of a mirror image, both in conviction as well as in the task of imparting his vision, Onetti as an artist makes it a matter to be *shown* rather than *told;* he dramatizes rather than tells. By the use of this technique the reader partakes of the vision and the task. We are let into the consciousness of a character-narrator and thus attain some degree of identification, some common ground with that narrator through whose perspective the experiences of the story are filtered. Our becoming "accomplices" to the narrator-hero's consciousness lends meaning, and what Coleridge called "suspension of disbelief," to what we witness. The apparent invisibility or absence of the author, furthermore, removes any obstacle between us and the narrator or the story he "tells." If the author were to assume the task of revealing Linacero's consciousness on the other hand, our normal inclination would be to ask, "Well, how do you know?"; in which case the story would lose its credibility or "suspension of disbelief."

The "I" as a subjective point of view in narration has its limitations, however, especially for a writer like Onetti whose vision eventually reaches cosmic proportions. An author who avails himself of this limited technique surrenders his channels of information to the narrator-protagonist and thus forfeits the narrative vantage points except for that of the singular "I." The story is reduced to a single experience or experiencing mechanism; "the protagonist narrator, therefore, is limited almost entirely to his own thoughts, feelings, and perceptions. Similarly, the angle of view is that of the fixed center."[10]

It is not surprising, therefore, that Onetti should abandon this narrative technique after his first work. This change, however, has its thematic implications as well as technical ones. With *Tierra de nadie,* the human condition, which Eladio Linacero symbolizes, now is generalized to collective proportions, that is, to the human community as a whole. This, of course, implies multiplicity.

III   Tierra de nadie

If Onetti is to remain faithful to the principles which guided his technique of point of view in the narration of his first work, he can no longer adhere to the same technique. A single consciousness cannot experience or relate the predicament of the collectivity; one being can only metaphorically symbolize it. If he attempts to narrate it, then he falls into the jeopardy of the deified author. The writer is, of course, constantly assuming omniscience, that is to say, regardless of how multiple a cosmos constitutes a work, it emanates from one man. But the author's art, as Lubbock points out, consists precisely of conveying to us the belief and convincing us that this is not the case.

Furthermore, the experience of *El pozo* has demonstrated that the "I" narration proves articulate only connotatively, only by implication. Eladio Linacero as a dramatized protagonist-narrator succeeds by example alone in making us understand his predicament. This procedure, of course, is what constitutes literature and art in general; we are given the "appearances of things" and not the things themselves. The writer, however, has to *show* us the human situation more convincingly, in a manner that transcends appearances, and in which the merely apparent is elevated to reality however phantasmal this reality might be. *Tierra de nadie* is such an attempt. We *see* a world and feel that we are experiencing it through our own consciousness instead of that of a narrator-protagonist. The eye, or peephole in this case, is impersonal. We are confronted with no one except the world of the novel and ourselves. The angle of view is impersonal, cold, thoroughly objective, and in the fragmented and disorderly situations and events the reader is the only fixed locus and center of consciousness.

The stillness in space (in the object world) and in chronometric time of which I spoke earlier extends beyond the descriptive process of isolated object or human characters who are objectified (as are Oscar in bed and Larsen's hand on the door in the opening pages) through a mechanical perspective. The narrative flow (there must be some if the story is to unfold) and progression of changing angles of vision move in an equally impersonal and mechanical fashion. What flows in the narrative, the mobile element, is not the world of the novel, not the city and its objective reality, but the reader and his eye like in a gallery of still-life scenes or before a multidimensional mural.

Tierra de nadie is composed of segments which consist of passages ranging from a paragraph to a few pages, and these in turn constitute sections. Sixty-one of these sections make up the work. The narrative movement from one fragment to the next and from one section to the following one represents a change of focus from one part of the city to another as well as a transference to a new thread of the disjointed narrative. In these movements the narrating perspective does not abandon the scrutinizing eye of a mechanical pointer. On the contrary, mechanical objects within the narrative become the carrying agents of the shifting focus and visual angle. The most striking example is to be found early in the novel. This shift is from the building stained with the hues of the red neon light of the opening scene to the office of Diego Aránzuru in some other part of the city. The movement between these two points is borne by the telephone call Larsen is putting through from his building to the office. Our perspective travels with the electrical signals sent through the copper wires, and we find ourselves in a new scene which opens up a new narrative trajectory, again to be abandoned with no conclusive summation of what it means to the story of the novel as a whole. The transition occurs in this manner:

The black nape was peppered with dandruff. He leaned on the railing of the corridor while Larsen was dialing the telephone.

In the empty hall, the sign Diego E. Aránzuru in black letters on the door's glass pane. Inside, a reflection of light filtering through the curtain, soft waves of music that descended from the bar on the eleventh floor. Vibrantly, the telephone's ringing began. (*oc*, 85)

The bearer of the movement is the telephone. The seeing eye which gives us our point of view continues to be a mechanical sensory agent. We approach the scene audiovisually and from the outside, gradually penetrating inwards.

The syntax of this passage is of special interest. With the exception of tense, the dry, nonemotional description of the scene is strikingly similar to stage directions for the cinema or the theater. What we have observed is a photograph or a projected movie scene, in this case with music in the background, the music from the eleventh floor, "soft waves" ("leves ondas") of music whose levity is to be shattered by the cicadalike sound of the telephone. At this point the scene is abandoned, and the preceding one is taken up again. There is no commentator, no author, nor anyone who might speak for him to reflect some connection, to give the reader some abstract generalization which would tie the significance of the two scenes together. This ultimate clarification is worked into the narrative itself; it is dramatized. We know why the phone call occurs because of the laconic and insinuating but not explicit dialogue between Larsen and Oscar in the preceding scene. This absence of such a narrator commentator holds true for the entire work.

In *Tierra de nadie* the objectivization of the subjective is achieved by implacably objective means. The sensors which filter or direct our view and perception are mechanical. The problem of identification with the narrative voice and of establishing a common ground with an intermediary narrator is eliminated. This is pure "unmediated realism," as pure as the cinema's or that of a scene which we might happen upon on some street corner. Authorial selection and editorship is without a doubt as present in this case as in any work of literature. The voice and seeing eye, however, are dehumanized to the extent that we do not identify them with the all-knowing author. This dehumanization of the narrative voice and eye emanates primarily from two sources: one, the impersonal and anonymous voice, the other, the pervasive and ubiquitous eye which is capable of transporting our visual perception everywhere simultaneously without recognition of physical or temporal barriers.

Tierra de nadie does not have what James calls a "central intelligence" or "the reader's friend." The coherence of the narrative comes from mirror images which are reflected in the various scenes from one fragment to another and with no particular order, sequence, or regularity. The interpenetrating fragmentation of the narrative flow is akin to a technique commonly identified with John Dos Passos. In *Manhattan Transfer*, however, counterpoint consists of parallel structures that never really converge except at the abstract plane of theme and the reader's deductive reflection. The parallelism does not exist in *Tierra de nadie*. The structure here is founded on a simultaneity achieved by means of the ubiquitous camera eye and the objective language which carry the flow of the narrative from one locus to another. As is the case with the work of Dos Passos, however, a full comprehension of Onetti's novel depends upon its being read in its entirety; a coherence is achieved from viewing the work as a whole. The reader is charged with the obligation of unifying all the segments and integrating them. Although *Tierra de nadie* is deficient in many respects (the simultaneity is not always attained), it represents an impressive technical undertaking and achievement on the part of the author of

El pozo, and a pioneering undertaking in the history of the Latin American novel. By his own admission, Vargas Llosa and other new novelists found inspiration for their narrative technique in these early efforts of Juan Carlos Onetti. The brand of realism and the method of cold objective portrayal practiced by the Peruvian novelist, especially in the opening scenes of *La casa verde,* attest to this debt.

IV   Para esta noche

Para esta noche has a traditional narrative structure, while at the same time it incorporates more modern techniques. Faulkner's influence is obvious and perhaps somewhat heavy-handed. Unlike *Tierra de nadie,* this work has a coherent story to relate from the very beginning. It is the story of a city (Buenos Aires) under the terror of a military siege and the inescapable destinies it has inflicted upon those of the opposition. Emir Rodríguez-Monegal points out that Onetti's novel, written on the eve of Perón's takeover in 1945, anticipated the terror which was to reign only two years after the novel's publication.

With respect to narrative point of view, *Para esta noche* represents a new trajectory in Onetti's work which will later evolve and produce the masterful technique of *Los adioses* and *Para una tumba sin nombre.* The technical novelty is the narration of the same events and circumstances from two or more points of view, by two or more narrators to the point where what is narrated becomes a different story.

The narrative of *Para esta noche* unfolds on two contrasting but complementary levels: that of the protagonist and that of the antagonist, Ossorio and Morasán. Onetti practices a rather amateurish metonymical use of characters by giving them a function of contrasting good and evil. Thus, their locus is moral as well as narrative. Ossorio emerges as the fated and hopeless incarnation of good helplessly fighting the evil forces of Morasán. The narration, however, is by no means limited to these two points of view. There is an ever-present anonymous voice which moderates and fills in between the monologues that pass through the characters' consciousness. These "interior monologues" come from every character, minor or major, in the novel. One could say then that everyone in the novel has a voice in the narration, each one articulating his own sphere of experience.

There is no overt intervention on the part of the author within these spheres even when the world experienced in these is narrated impersonally by the anonymous voice. We receive no marginal explanations on the actions or thought processes of the characters. The situations are left to speak dramatically for themselves. Although this is technically the case, it is not altogether true. There is a *tone* in the narrative, a tone which discloses the author's hand. Onetti cannot disguise his sympathies and antipathies toward the character-narrators. The narration of Morasán and about Morasán, therefore, has a constant one-sided sinister quality to it. And we cannot help but feel a "complicity" between Ossorio and the anonymous, impersonal narrator. Such authorial failure in detachment runs the risk of stating oversimplified dichotomies and of essayistic narration, which are not entirely lacking in the novel.

As a whole, the work is by no means among the best of Onetti, and the better part of the novel consists of the first four parts. This segment is the cabaret scene which the reader witnesses from primarily two distinct points of view: that of Ossorio and that of Morasán. The two focus in each case on the same objects, situations, and events. From each we get a completely different version and thus a different story which, when collated by the reader, forms a complete picture of the scene. The claustrophobic cabaret becomes a microcosm in which the good, the bad, and the indifferent prowl and gesticulate. It is an actual microcosm of the city, for like the metropolis, the cabaret and everyone within it are also sequestered and under siege by the lugubrious and ominous thugs of Morasán.

The fact that the novel's narrative flow is subjected to two internal parallel narrative foci indicates a vacillation; Onetti might be uncertain about his narrative technique. (This "vacillation" recurs, and will be intentionally exploited by the author to produce a work like *Para una tumba sin nombre*.) The forking of the narration is not and should not be viewed simply as a function by which the author is segregating moral and philosophical positions. The divergence within the work should be considered as Onetti's dramatization and functional articulation of the technical problem of narrating a story. In other words, the narrative technique and point of view that a writer chooses determine the nature of a work and its story. This problem of uncertainty is not by any means new or original with Onetti. The Brazilian, Machado de Assis constructed his works in the nineteenth century by exploiting the dilemma. Though *Para esta noche* is not a perfect work, it serves its function within the developmental process of the novelist, and it also foreshadows a major work like *El astillero*. For the critic *Para esta noche* is useful since it helps understand the technical antecedents of Onetti's masterpiece, the fruition of a twenty-year career.

V La vida breve

It is with his next work, *La vida breve,* that Onetti comes into his own. With this novel he succeeds in molding the inheritance from Faulkner and Dos Passos into his own style and technique. The technical carry-overs from *El pozo, Tierra de nadie,* and *Para esta noche* are also definitely present. Their use in *La vida breve,* however, acquires subtlety, and the author's hand is much less obvious to the reader.

Like the two preceding works, *La vida breve* has a multiple narrative structure. The novel is told on three simultaneous but distinct and interrelated planes in addition to the author's third-person narration. Narrative time is erratic and shifting between present and past according to the psychological associations of the narrator-protagonist. These three levels are that of Juan María Brausen, of Arce, and of Díaz Grey. Since the last two characters are "ectoplasms" of the first, all three narrative planes fuse into one to be refracted in the psyche of Juan María Brausen.

With *La vida breve* Onetti returns to take up where he left off with *El pozo.* The two works which intervene could be considered experimental. In his fourth work the author returns to the protagonist as narrator as well as assuming a narrative role himself. This time, however, he gives his protagonist's imagination free rein and allows himself to explore and exploit all the possibilities that his new technique in narrative point of view has to offer. Whereas the basic premise of *El pozo's* method was that man is singular, an alienated and individuated consciousness which can reveal itself only through that existential circumstance, the premise of *La vida breve* seems to hold that man is one but at the same time many, a multiple being, consisting of a series of individuated and alienated selves. The narration of the work commences from here, and its technique of point of view proceeds from this position. The series of short lives which, as the title indicates, a man lives, become the source of the several levels of narration and points of view through which the world unfolds. Each sphere of experience operating in Brausen's psyche produces a center of reference, a voice and a narrative locus. Whether imagined or "actual," each locus becomes equally significant.

Luis Harss states, citing Onetti, that the author feels more at home when he becomes one with his character-narrators, a technique he has cultivated since his very first work: "Passing himself off as his narrator is a favorite Onetti device: 'I feel freer, more like myself, working this way' he says."[11] The fusion of the author into his protagonist-narrator in *La vida breve* is consistent with the case of *El pozo*. But the Onetti of 1950 has developed as man and author since the writing of *El pozo*. Analogously, the protagonist-narrator of *La vida breve* is more complex and his horizons are broader. It is, let us say, as if a greater writer than Faulkner were writing *The Sound and the Fury* and included Faulkner as a protagonist-narrator who was compelled to become simultaneously Benjy, Quinten, Jason, and Dilsey. Yet the relationship of Onetti to *La vida breve* and his work in general remains the same to the point that Emir Rodríguez-Monegal states, with respect to *Los adioses*, that "The witness-narrator writes like Onetti." The same critic also observes, and I paraphrase from the Spanish, that even though a work like *La vida breve* clearly distinguishes between the point of view of the author and the narrator's point of view, there is no doubt that the author and the protagonist share the same attitude toward creation. If Onetti creates Brausen by an act of the imagination and interpolates him into the real world through the means of a novel, Brausen creates Juan María Arce and later Díaz Grey through a similar act. The only difference, barely important from the narrative point of view, is the unique world of fiction, that is to say, the literary ambit of the book.[12] Furthermore, if we approach the relationship of author to character in a Pirandellian or Borgesian manner, we can say that there really is no difference whatsoever between Brausen and Juan Carlos Onetti since his reality, not only as author but as a creative man, is derived from the phantasmal creatures of his fiction.

The narrative progression of the work (not a linear, chronological progression by any means) resembles an outward passage from the center through layers of an onion, through a series of mirrors, each representing a narrative point of view on a new fictional plane. The "movement" is outward, originating in Brausen's consciousness (even before Brausen, Onetti's consciousness) and moving stepwise to new planes represented by Arce and Díaz Grey. Thus with each new plunge through the looking glass we are confronted with a new objectivization, a new "concretization" of Brausen's subjective world. A new subjectivity which of itself proceeds to unfold before our eyes is represented by these objectivized planes. Implicit is a paradox that with each move of Brausen's subjectivity to make itself objective, we are removed one more step into the phantasmal reality of fiction. Thus we witness an attempt to reach reality through a constant plunging into unreality.

Narrative point of view in *La vida breve* acquires a new objectivity, a new set of criteria with each movement. The narrative, nonetheless, does not become unrealistic to the reader who must follow these metamorphic transitions, for he is not abandoned to any incongruities that would lead him to question the point of view, the focus which is guiding him and which reveals these multiple worlds of "unreality." By the end of the work the story establishes its internal reality and its own criteria of objectivity.

VI *The third person narrator*

After *La vida breve* and with the founding of the mythical Santa María, emanation of Juan María Brausen's fantasy, Onetti opts for a third-person anonymous narrative voice that never lets us forget to whom it pertains, whether it speaks for itself or for the characters. Onetti has been frequently criticized for his tonality, which becomes inseparable and undifferentiated from either the thoughts, words, or narration of his characters. In *Juntacadáveres* Díaz Grey speaks and thinks with the same intonations as the anonymous third-person narrator; similarly in *El astillero* the author's voice blends with Junta Larsen's consciousness and words. Perhaps this could be called authorial intrusion. What we have is an overt complicity staged by the author between himself, his characters, and narrator in the tone and point of view of the story. If the context did not guide us in a given situation, we would not be able to differentiate between the author's voice and the characters' consciousness. In both cases the narration comes to us through an indifferent and detached point of view, through a resigned voice that has surrendered to skepticism. Compare, for example, the opening of two successive paragraphs from *Juntacadáveres;* the first voice belongs to Díaz Grey, the second is that of the author-narrator:

To know who I am. Nothing, zero, an irrevocable company, a presence for others. For me, nothing. Forty years, a lost life; a way of stating why I can not imagine it won.

Saber quien soy. Nada, cero, una compañía irrevocable, una presencia para los demás. Para mí, nada. Cuarenta años, vida perdida; una forma de decir porque no puedo imaginarla ganada.

Alone in the square of Santa María, shortly after turning forty, in a night of
that summer in which the city was filled with jazmines. It was around the
time the government fell. He could tend to a birth, mend bones, diagnose
cancer, clean wounds, prescribe placebos and morphine.

Solitario en la plaza de Santa María, poco después de cumplir los cuarenta
años, en una noche de aquel verano en que la ciudad se llenó de jazmines.
Era allá por el tiempo del golpe de estado. Podía atender un parto, unir
huesos, diagnosticar un cáncer, limpiar heridas, recetar pantopán y morfina.

Reading through these passages, it is difficult to distinguish what
the focal center of reference is in each excerpt. There is no shift in
the visual angle or in the tonal quality of the narrating voice. Both
narrators articulate, it seems, looking into the distance, reflectively,
hopelessly.

Having found a cosmos all his own to elaborate, the author-
narrator blends himself into its life and the lives of its inhabitants. I
do not think, however, it is a matter of authorial omniscience with
Onetti but rather an empathy for his characters which makes it hard
for him to detach himself from his fictitious world.

Nevertheless, within the cosmogony of Santa María, Juan Carlos
Onetti has created two short novels that attest to his technical
mastery of narrative point of view and which might be his way of
rebuffing those critics who see his undifferentiated narration as a
shortcoming. The technique of blending tone in *Los adioses* (1954)
and *Para una tumba sin nombre* (1959) seems to be an intentional
choice on the part of Onetti.

VII *Intimations of Henry James*

From the perspective of narrative point of view, *Los adioses*
represents a rather new way of presenting the narrative. Like most
of his fiction, it is a novel which explores creativity on two
simultaneous planes, the theoretical and the practical. The problem
is dramatized through an astute use of ambiguity. A "detached"
character within the story witnesses and presents the events to the
reader through the sordid angle of his point of view and of his personal bias. It is not until the end of the novel that we discover the
unreliability of the narrator through a variation, an authorial,
narrative correction which exposes the sordidness of the narrator's
mind. In addition, the final revelation proves an embarrassment for

the reader who, willingly or not, has been in complicity with the perverse narrator in the creation of the tale.

The story takes place in the hills of Cordoba, where victims of tuberculosis seek to be cured or, as is the specific case in *Los adioses*, retire to give in to the inevitable. A nameless ex-athlete arrives in the town as a patient. His arrival and life are related to us by the owner of the general store who is witness to all the comings and goings of the town. Our only view of the afflicted basketball player comes from the eyewitness testimony of this local grocer-postmaster who obviously is in an advantageous position to know what he is talking about. The owner of the grocery-bar-restaurant-post-office establishment, situated in the heart of the town, has been witness to the life (and death) of this resort for many years. It is natural for the reader to take him at his word. Accepting him in his role of inside narrator, a character within the story and on-the-spot observer, we give him our support and eager ear for what he has to tell. As a witness, however, the grocer does not adhere to the outward appearance of things but ventures into speculations and affirmations which go beyond what he sees. Nor does the reader feel inclined to question these assertions. On the contrary, he accepts them readily, which in turn becomes a way of urging the narrator on, for his assertions lend the story some degree of interest and intrigue. Once subjected to the interest evoked by the witness' narration, the reader does not for a moment think or even entertain the notion that the author might be withholding information, which is actually the case all along. Thus, both the observer and through him the reader have created a viable story and given its participants a human destiny.

Besides the key position which the narrator occupies within the situation of the story, there is another technical mechanism which convinces the reader of the apparent validity of the narrator's observations and of his reliability. I am referring to the minutely "objective" and detailed manner with which the witness-narrator relates the gestures and particulars of his subject. It is an objectivity with which we are already familiar from Onetti's earlier works. Beginning with the opening paragraph we are subjected to these seemingly acute objective observations:

The first time the man entered the store, I would have liked to have seen nothing but his hands: slow, intimidated, and clumsy, moving without faith, long and not tanned as yet, begging forgiveness for their disinterested behavior . . . I would have liked to have seen nothing but his hands, it would have been enough to have seen them when I gave him the change for the hundred pesos and the fingers clutched the bills, tried to arrange them and, suddenly, resolutely made it into a flattened ball and prudently hid it in a jacket pocket. . . . (*oc*, 717)

Reading the novel for the first time and unaware of its conclusion, the reader would see in the grocer nothing but an objective viewer who does not miss a thing of what he is witnessing. After completing the story, however, and returning to these passages, the reader becomes aware of something strange about this supposedly "objective" narration. It is in the final analysis a selective objectivity, qualified with very personal adjectives. Onetti might be demonstrating the impossibility of total objectivity on the part of any human being, layman, writer, narrator, or author. The human senses cannot experience everything simultaneously. What we do perceive fragmentarily, partially, is not accidental, and having acquired these perceptions, we can no longer remain as we were prior to our having experienced them. The perceptions are also transformed, personalized, and metamorphosed by our human condition.

On a second critical reading of *Los adioses* and with the ending in mind, we realize that the apparent objectivity of the witness-narrator is anything but objective. We discover that the narrator is seeing not merely a pair of hands belonging to a sick man, but rather hands without faith, hands that excuse themselves for their disinterestedness, hands that are capable of resoluteness and of prudence. Thus, the detached and disinterested point of view that related the story now is revealed to us as a judgmental voice whose qualifying adjectives speak louder than its uncommitted substantives. This technical oddity is the key to the work: "The point of view of a witness, seemingly objective, but extremely subjective in actuality, is the key to the ambiguity."[13] However, the ambiguity does not appear as such until the end of the work when the "true" story emerges.

Through a couple of letters that the narrator of *Los adioses* has kept from the ailing basketball player we learn that the athlete's correspondents are his daughter and second wife. These are the same women whose visits have led our eyewitness narrator to construct the intrigue of a multiple amorous involvement. Astounded and awed by his discovery, the grocer-narrator does not admit defeat. He copes with the revealed facts in this manner: "It would be enough for me to place my recent discovery at the beginning of the story in order for everything to become simple and foreseeable. I felt full of power, as if the man and the girl, and also the woman and the child, had been born of my will to live what I had determined. I was smiling as I thought about this again, while I was being reconciled with forgiving the basketball champion's final avidity" (*oc*, 768 - 69). There is no reason why he should accept defeat, for as it is, *his story* stands and *his* version, the contents of *his* narrative point of view, is what comprises Onetti's novel. With some incidental differences in a couple of facts, the circumstances are still the same. No one ever expects a story to be "true" or factual. Why should it be expected of this one? Literature is after all a hypothetical conjecture whose subject is life and the universe. As Borges would say, "Perhaps universal history is the history of the diverse intonation of a few metaphors."[14] The grocer-storyteller then is entitled to his own intonations, sordid or dubious as they may be. We always have the writer who authored him and who might reveal the varied nature of these intonations.

Los adioses is the dramatization of the creative process. What we witness is the creation of a story and subsequently the reality and life on which the story has been based. The ambiguity then becomes an integral part of the creative process. To paraphrase Rodríguez-Monegal once again, Onetti uses ambiguity because his vision of the world is ambiguous, because his concept of the universe rests on the duality of criteria which allows the greatest of sordidness (for the spectator, the witness) to contain a charge of unredeemed poesy (for the patient).[15]

As questionable or sordid as the witness-creator and narrator might be, he is a reflection of the man and the artistic practice which engendered him. And, although Onetti does not engage in literary theory outside his fictional work, as many other writers are wont to do, *Los adioses* is a clear indication that he does theorize about his art. His theorizing in *Los adioses* deals with the problem of perspective and narrative point of view. The same is the case with his next work, *Para una tumba sin nombre*, which appears five years later and is even more self-conscious and reflective than *Los adioses*.

Para una tumba sin nombre brings us back to the heart of Santa María. The narrator, Dr. Díaz Grey, is constantly conscious of his role as narrator-chronicler. He is best described by this nomenclature, for his task is not simply to narrate but to document, to put before us various versions and segments of a story not primarily his own. He, as a center of reference, supplies the cohesiveness of the narrative. Thus, as a "narrator," he does not hold the privilege of an inside view or of a registering consciousness; rather, he conveys a series of divergent points of view of the same situation within the story. He might be called, in Henry James' terminology, "the reader's friend."

The story which Díaz Grey attempts to compile for us, in the manner of a puzzle or a collage, is that of a young and dissolute woman and her billy goat, symbolic alternately of the *cabrón* ("pimp") and of a scapegoat. Her story, like her life, becomes the story of Marcos Bergner, of Ambrosio, and most eminently, of Jorge Malabia, before it becomes the story of Díaz Grey, of Juan Carlos Onetti, and, finally, the reader's. The young woman, Rita, uses the billy goat as a ploy in her solicitations at a railroad station of Buenos Aires. Jorge Malabia feels that he has a rightful claim to her because when he was younger he would spy on her and Marcos Bergner (his sister-in-law's brother) in their erotic entanglements. Jorge exploits Rita with an amoral and passionless urge. Although he is aware that she is dying of consumption, he continues to exploit her prostitution, despite the fact that he could support both her and himself. Finally, he brings her back to Santa María where she will occupy a nameless tomb. Nameless, because as we learn from Tito, his roommate at Buenos Aires, Jorge invents a cousin of Rita and dubs her the victim of the disease in order to ease his own conscience.

The narrative sequence of the story is reversed. We are first given the culmination of the events and then the circumstances and situations which lead to the conclusion. The narration of the incidents which explain the end of the story are revealed to us piecemeal, and proceed from numerous sources of varying distance from the focal center or principal situation. These sources become informants or agents of the primary narrator Díaz Grey. Thus, the narrative is "polyfacetic" with a multiplicity of perspectives shown or dramatized in themselves and filtered through the recipient point of view of Díaz Grey, who offers his own version by means of a compilation of the multiple perspectives. The informants range from the employee of the funeral home to Godoy, to Jorge Malabia, who is the primary informant and a secondary narrator, to Tito Perotti, Malabia's roommate. Each of the individual perspectives represents a potential story in itself. *Para una tumba sin nombre* then could technically be considered a multiple version of *Los adioses*. In this case, however, we have Díaz Grey who, along with the reader, seems to be aware of the possible divergent stories which could result from a given situation and a specific set of facts. Jorge Malabia, who emerges at times as a narrator, not narrating to us, but to Díaz Grey (but for our benefit, of course), seems also to have some cognizance of his role as storyteller and narrator. Thus, we listen in as he tells Díaz Grey, "I am not demanding that you take note of this or that; I simply suggest it. When I ask that you notice something I am not helping you to understand the story in the least; but perchance those suggestions might be useful to you in moving closer to my comprehension of the story, to my story" (*oc*, 1006).

Malabia's methodological interjection during the course of his confessions to Díaz Grey is, I believe, speaking for Onetti. It represents a concern on the author's part for narrative objectivity of which *Para una tumba sin nombre* seems to be an incarnation. What Onetti offers is a series of *sugerencias* ("suggestions") as the story is being structured. Seemingly none are his own. Yet, since he is the author, we well know that they are all his, as is the story. Nonetheless, as Malabia claims for his version, there is little or no emphasis given to any aspect or to any particular perspective of the story.

As a "reader's friend" and the author's spokesman, Díaz Grey does not refrain from judging Malabia both in his motives and in his style of narration. By giving Díaz Grey this power, Onetti the author washes his hands of Malabia's part in the story and the narrative, another means by which the author detaches himself from the story or any responsibility for the words and motives of his character-narrators. Díaz Grey tells us, for example, parenthetically: "It must have been because he felt pity swelling within him or because he was not able to hide that it was essentially out of pity—and its impure form, remorse—that he had come to tell me the story. In spite of everything, apart from everything, apart from the pleasure of an entire night in the first person, at center stage, apart from the intoxication of being the god of what he evoked. It must have been for that reason that he made recourse to diverse weaknesses: irony, vanity, hardness" (*oc*, 1008). The passage is ironical in itself since it reflects back on the author. Malabia, who is the subject of the passage, is after all a trajectory, a tangent in Onetti's mind. Later, Jorge Malabia admits to Díaz Grey: "I could be wrong when I think that my story is infinitely more important than the story. I could tell you the story in two or three minutes and then you construct your own story and perhaps . . ."(*oc*, 1009 - 10).

The magus is showing off his masks, for I believe that the words uttered by Jorge Malabia here are an attestation of Onetti's own view of literature and perspective in his craft. It is a dramatization of the dialectic between life in its primary form and life in art. Within the context of the work, it is Jorge Malabia's Pirandellian self-assertion that he too is an emanation of art, engaged in narrating a point of view which is capable of becoming an independent work of art, a story in itself. It is his way of reminding Díaz Grey that he is not to be taken as "a slice of life" in its natural, crude, and amorphous state. This is a very Jamesian affirmation on Onetti's part that art is infinitely richer and more perfect than life. As was the case in *Los adioses*, it could be interpreted to mean that the mere choice in the narrative point of view within the process of transforming life into art, implies the nature and essence of the final product, the fruit of the art itself. Onetti, again as in *Los adioses*, has chosen a specific narrator and narrative point of view which is the central reference to the work. In *Para una tumba sin nombre*, however, he has placed his central reference, the primary but incomplete narrative focus of Díaz Grey, in apposition to various other points of reference and perspective. Thus, although we might consider this work as a story of Onetti, it is more (or perhaps less) than that: it is the makings and the making of a story and not, as Jorge says, "the story." Besides, the existence of a story which is "the story" seems to be dubious. Everyone considers his version to be the definitive and by far the most important one. Thus, Tito, not unlike Jorge, tells Díaz Grey, "And now I remember the funniest, or most important part of the story, the true story, the one I am telling you" (*oc*, 1041). And, in their final encounter Jorge tells Díaz Grey that the whole thing is an invention which he and Tito undertook as a challenge and would prefer to leave it at that: "Let's leave it that way, as a story which we invented among ourselves, including you." To which Díaz Grey adds, "that could be told in a different way another thousand times. But maybe it's true that it isn't worth it" (*oc*, 1044).

Everyone participating in the work, reader, author, characters, and narrator, is consciously aware of the phantasmal nature of what is involved, the story, its narration, and even the reality which engendered them all. Onetti, integrating himself into the voice of Díaz Grey, concludes the novel saying: "The only thing that counts is that when I finished writing it I felt at peace, sure of having achieved the most important thing that could be expected from this sort of task: I had accepted a challenge, I had converted into victory at least one of the daily defeats" (*oc*, 1046).

In conclusion, one could say that a work like *Para una tumba sin nombre* is an Onettian version of *The Whole Family: A Novel by Twelve Authors* (1908) written by Henry James and eleven coauthors, each writing a chapter with a different central intelligence and a new perspective on the same events. As Wayne Booth points out, one's interest in such a work is in point of view rather than in what the point of view reveals. Perhaps this is what Jorge means when he considers his own story to be infinitely more interesting than the story which is merely a matter of a couple of minutes and nothing more.

CHAPTER 5

The Thickening Plot

A S R. S. Crane convincingly argues, any novel is a composite of three basic elements: the things that are imitated or rendered, namely, human beings and their world; a linguistic medium in which they are presented; and, finally, a manner or technique of imitation (of rendering).[1] Plot is a particular temporal synthesis of the elements of action, character, and thought that make up the writer's invention. According to Professor Crane's supposition and derived definition, plot evolves and revolves around the first basic element of any work, that is to say, around human beings, and more specifically, around the protagonist or principal characters within a given work. Particularizing the definition even further, Norman Friedman sees plot as "a group of two or more episodes effecting a completed process of change in the main character," the end of a plot being "to represent some completed process of change in the protagonist for the sake of the sequence of emotions which that process evokes in the reader."[2]

As a synthetic formula, consisting of action, character, and thought, the plot takes on varying characteristics in proportion to the predominance or absence of each one of these component elements. Their degree of influence as a synthesizing principle in that process of "completed change in the protagonist" determines the type of plot. Thus we emerge with three basic types, namely, plots of action (Friedman's term is "fortune"), plots of character, and plots of thought. In the first, the "completed change" occurs in the situation of the protagonist, as determined and effected by character and thought; in the second, it occurs in the moral character of the protagonist, precipitated by action and made manifest in thought; and in the third, this process of change is in the thought of the protagonist, and consequently, his feelings and human condition, as directed by character and action. Norman Friedman adds a series of subcategories to Crane's basic threefold classification. I shall not enumerate these here, but simply draw upon them as it becomes necessary.

The most active principle in plot is change. The recipient of this process of change is the human factor within the work, and it is the protagonists who are most affected. Thus, it is inevitable that I should once again be speaking of the characters within the novels of Onetti. Whereas previously I had primarily considered the author's technique of characterization, my focus now turns to the characters themselves and to what happens to them, to the permutations given of their lives, moral character, and thoughts within the span of a work, and frequently (since many of Onetti's men and women move from novel to novel with the author) the turns which their lives take during the course of these novelistic transmigrations. I shall begin where I left off at the end of the last chapter, with Jorge Malabia, Díaz Grey, and *Para una tumba sin nombre*.

I   Para una tumba sin nombre

This novel lends itself to commencing our discussion of plot and plot structure for various reasons. It is first of all an episodic work and, since two or more episodes which facilitate a completed process of change within the protagonist make for a plot, *Para una tumba sin nombre* makes for a natural starting point. Second, the author does not entwine these episodes in such a way that they would blend into each other, giving the effect of a unified totality and concealing the edges of beginning and ending of each episode. On the contrary, he intentionally allows us to witness the collating process by which his narrative takes form. Last, and most significantly, in this work the completed process of change is documented for us by the author's narrative agent or "reader's friend," Dr. Díaz Grey.

Although this short novel revolves around the life of the dissolute Rita, who is destined to occupy the tomb that gives the work its title, the true protagonist is Jorge Malabia. The novel has been described as the story of Jorge's sentimental education, in which the young protagonist crosses over into adulthood carrying with him an obsession which is self-provoked: the physical conquest of Rita. Jorge, furthermore, asserts his claim to the work and views himself as its central protagonist when he tells Díaz Grey, that of all the versions *his* "story is infinitely the more important one."

Jorge's words reveal a great deal. That is, if he were as aware and

cognizant of what he is saying as are Onetti or the critical reader,
Jorge would know that in the dichotomy between "my story" and
"the story" he is delineating the distinction between the work's
plot and its argument. "La historia," the story, as he says, could be
recounted in two or three minutes. This is the work's argument,
consisting of the skeletal résumé of events. It does not, however, include or consider means, causes, effects, and ends. Nor does it consider the characters' motivations and the changes they undergo in
the process of pursuing their goals. These elements are precisely
what comprises "mi historia" ("my story") the plot of the novel
which is Jorge's confrontation with life and its consequences upon
his moral character, thoughts, and feelings. Indeed, as Jorge
asserts, "his story" is the infinitely more important part of the
novel. Obviously, then, Jorge emerges as the protagonist of the
work, because he is the one who is subjected to the major change,
and it is his situation and character around which all else in the
plot revolves. It is Jorge's "sentimental education" that lies at the
heart of the story.

The change and progressive transformations that take place in
Jorge's moral character are documented, step by step, by Díaz
Grey. Throughout the novel the young man's situation ("fortune")
remains constant; it persists even during the moments of conflict
and after the denouement. The younger son of a provincial family,
Jorge is all along sustained by his family in his financial and practical needs. What slight change the reader might note in his mode
of life, like his thoughts, is a function of the alterations which occur
to his character.

The flow of events signal a maturation or a coming-of-age for the
protagonist. It is a uniquely Onettian attainment of maturity,
however. Unlike Ike McCaslin of Faulkner's "The Bear" or
Stephen Dedalus of Joyce's *A Portrait of the Artist as a Young Man*,
Jorge Malabia abandons all vestiges of moral character upon coming of age. Ever since he was a child and spied on the erotic inter-
course of Rita and Marcos Bergner, he had felt a rightful claim
upon her. Later when she was the maid of his brother's demented
widow, Rita rejected Jorge's advances. Finally, hearing of her life-
style from Godoy, a middle-aged townsman who evokes a feeling of
indignation in him, Jorge, more than ever, is sexually obsessed with
Rita. The attainment of this goal, in the end, resolves his inner conflict, and he settles into an attitude of apathetic amorality, exploiting the prostitute woman as a means, physically as well as

financially, with a relish of which only Onetti's men are capable. Malabia abandons his studies while continuing to receive financial support from home. He turns over the money to some political cause for which he has no passion. He occupies his time lying in bed staring at the ceiling, awaiting the return of Rita and the billy goat. In his languishing, the protagonist surrenders the remaining vestiges of human dignity upon reaching adulthood and maturity. He has exchanged his moral character for a spurious manhood. In the end he comes to believe that, "I shall never be able to regret anything, because anything that I do can only be done if it is within the human possibilities" (*oc*, 1041).

A year after the burial of Rita, the death of the billy goat, and Jorge Malabia's "confessions" to Díaz Grey (upon which the latter constructs a viable story), Jorge returns to Díaz Grey for a variety of motives, chief of which is the amelioration of his gnawing conscience. During this encounter, Díaz Grey takes the occasion to observe the character of the protagonist and to pinpoint three transformations in Malabia which he reveals confidentially (in quotations) to the reader. As Jorge reads what Díaz Grey, after having witnessed the burial and heard the confessions of a year ago, had written, Díaz Grey observes the young man and articulates his thoughts to us: "There is something already, I thought. He learned to take himself seriously, not with the desperation and the sense of fatality of before, but calmly, without realizing his ridiculousness and self misery. Almost the same way in which his father and any of the men at the poker table of the Progreso Club take themselves seriously" (*oc*, 1026 - 27). "The second baseness is that the passion of rebellion has died in him, and he tried to substitute it with cynicism, which is within reach of any finished man . . ." (*oc*, 1028). Between the first observation (which seems to describe the attainment of a sort of manhood) and the second one, cynicism and an implication of apathy have crept in; for cynicism, we are told, is at the reach of any man, even one who is finished. And then the final comment: "The third baseness consists of the adult sin of believing *a posteriori* that irremediable acts need our permission" (*oc*, 1031). Worst of all, our protagonist has become subject to self-deception in the face of the irremediable and the inevitable.

At the time of this meeting, Jorge is twenty-five-years old and Díaz Grey recalls a young man in the throes of maturing: "Since the last time that we saw each other, I thought, he has been learning to judge, to not love any one, and that is a hard education.

But he had not as yet come to love himself, to accept himself. . . . He was at the age of fear; he protected himself with hardness and intolerance" (oc, 1024). The three changes that Díaz Grey observes do not permit the reader to make his own decision as to what kind of transformation the protagonist has undergone and, consequently what type of plot prevails within the work. We cannot rightfully say that the plot here is one of "maturation," for that has positive connotations; nor can we say that it is simply a "plot of degeneration," since the authorial judgment through the voice of Díaz Grey takes us further, as is evident above. We could, then, only agree with his judgment and call the plot one of pathetic "resignation."

Implicit in Díaz Grey's "objective" appraisal of Jorge is the realization that man must come to resignation. It seems to be inevitable in the Onettian world. After all, it is Díaz Grey, another resigned Onettian figure, who makes this observation and passes judgment on the human reality. A matured and seasoned character, his commentary attests to this inevitability.

This, then, is the plot of *Para una tumba sin nombre*, a character plot, a plot of "maturity," but more accurately, a plot of degeneration as manifested in that process of completed change in Jorge Malabia. Within the reaches of Onetti's vision of reality and of the human condition, the plot of the novel could be no other than what it is. Jorge Malabia and the author's world, in which he has briefly taken a part as a protagonist, are predestined by a metaphysics and an all-pervasive fate to precisely this kind of a plot.

The predestination and the factors which predetermined this fate can be easily documented in *Para una tumba sin nombre*. Their antecedents are revealed five years later in Onetti's novel *Juntacadáveres*. In this latter work, Jorge appears as a sensitive, perhaps overly sensitive, adolescent who composes verses. He eventually is dragged into an immoral relationship with the widow of his brother. The rightful protagonist is Junta Larsen, whose name partially gives the book its title. Jorge, however, also narrates his own thoughts and experiences. Though *Juntacadáveres* is posterior to *Para una tumba sin nombre* in date of composition and publication, the career of the protagonist originates in the more recent work. Thus, if we were to read *Juntacadáveres* first, as Emir Rodríguez-Monegal, editor of Onetti's *Obras completas*, has done precisely for this purpose, we would perceive a natural evolution of the plot and of Jorge Malabia's character. In *Juntacadáveres* the author has supplied us with the basis for a definite source of "inferential activity," to use R. S. Crane's terminology, which is in-dispensable to a writer for the success of his plot; the author is not through, after all, until the work is read and until he can evoke in the reader a desire to know what comes next and how it will all emerge or culminate.

In *Juntacadáveres* Jorge Malabia points to his end as the protagonist of *Para una tumba sin nombre* right after his first sex-ual contact with Julita, his brother's widow, when he reflects:

> —But you have never done it—Tito will repeat. You just can't know.
> And although I am sure that he has never done it either, I will accept, without letting on, that he is right. I will feel as if I am saying good-bye to them, that a world more impure than that of distracted friendship has trapped me and I can not know, for sure, until when. . . ." (*oc*, 816)

We also see his future foreshadowed by his attempt to abandon Santa María with Junta Larsen, which was aborted by the untimely suicide of Julita.

Jorge Malabia is not unique as a character who appears at a later stage in life in an early work and vice versa. Other Onettian protagonists and plots, unlike the nineteenth-century heroes that moved from novel to novel in a chronological sequence, have their origins in works published at a later date than when the reader was first introduced to them. This, of course, is a consequence of the closed-off world of Onetti's fiction. He has devised a cosmos ac-cording to his vision and goes on revealing its saga in segments—each of its parts capable of becoming entire fictional units in themselves, each of his world's inhabitants potentially a protagonist. Before venturing farther into this sealed-off cosmos of Santa María, however, I should like to return to the primeval work, *El pozo*.

II *Vicissitudes of a plot*

It has been said that an author writes essentially one work, and that the rest of his literary production is an elaboration of that work. It has also been said that "universal history is an infinite and sacred book that all men write and read and try to understand, and in which they too are written."[3] The first of these assertions may be applied to Juan Carlos Onetti's *El pozo*; the second, to the entirety of his work as a fragment of "universal history" in which the author is included as well. In his first novel, Onetti puts forth not only a vision of reality and a style of narration which set the prece-

dent for his subsequent works, but also the prototype for future
narrative structure or plot development.[4]

In a notebook which he kept for the purpose of jotting down
skeletal arguments of works he intended to write, Borges tells us
that Nathaniel Hawthorne recorded the plan for writing a dream
"which shall resemble the real course of a dream, with all its inconsistency, its eccentricities and aimlessness."[5] Eladio Linacero an-
nounces for Onetti a similar plan which has since materialized and
continues to fulfill itself. "It could also be a plan," Linacero tells us,
"to go on telling an 'event' and a dream" (oc, 51). The primordial
actor, the protagonist, of any dream is the dreamer. The phantasms
with which he populates his dream are projections of his reverie or
hallucinations and are multiplied versions of the somnolent
protagonist. It should not surprise us then that the characters who
inhabit and somnambulate within the realm of a writer's dreams
should show certain affinities to each other and a homogeneity
among themselves. They, after all, proceed from a single source.

The equation of literature with dreaming is not original either
with Hawthorne or with Juan Carlos Onetti. Not every writer will
accept being called a dreamer, however, including Eladio Linacero,
who states: "The curious thing is that if someone said that I was 'a
dreamer' it would bother me. It's absurd. I have lived like anyone
or more" (oc, 51). But Hawthorne and Onetti are among those
authors who see a very fine line separating life and dream and,
therefore, the frequently imperceivable difference between creating
lives and projecting dreams; or between living and dreaming. Like
Schopenhauer, who held "that life and dreams were pages from the
same book, and that to read them in their proper order was to live,
but to scan them at random was to dream," [6] Onetti, more than
Hawthorne (for the latter never fully developed his plan) is aware
that his task as writer and as a man is one of constantly "scanning."
He has founded a cosmos analogous to that of his "real" life and
continues to scan its annals and pages.

Usually, within the confines of any given work, the characters
simulate living, for the author sees to it that the "pages" from the
"book" unfold in "their proper order." This is not always the case
in Onetti's novels; his personages also become subject to "scanning" and, therefore, to dreaming, thus reflecting their author in
his activity of embuing them with life. For this reason, in Onetti's
works plots of character dominate, while plots of action occupy a
secondary position.

Insofar as the existence of a plot is dependent upon change in some aspect of the protagonist's life, some of Onetti's novels could be said to fall short of having a plot, unless it be a plot of apathy or resignation. In such "plotless" works the only change in the character's life consists of his having traversed certain episodes and a span of time to find himself, in the end, back where he started with the same resigned attitude and more convinced than ever of his original outlook. Onetti begins his career with this kind of plot and, in many ways, sets the precedent for subsequent works.

As an author who subjects his protagonist to the same situation and somnolent undertaking as he himself undergoes, Onetti is not cryptic about the part which his own fantasizing has in the life of his characters. Ángel Rama claims that Linacero is a thinly disguised representation of the author.[7] Nor is this the only such instance of self-representation in Onetti's work. We could say, then, that to analyze the plots of Onetti's novels is to follow the transmutations the author himself has undergone, since he is, as it were, the true protagonist of his own *oeuvre*.

In Onetti, the culmination of each plot represents a more complex and more replete version of the preceding one. Thus, each work points to the one that came before it. In terms of transformation of the protagonists, the plot seems to remain the same in type, with the works in which it evolves representing a new and more elaborate version of their forerunner. This constant harping back, as well as the unchanging thematic preoccupation have earned Onetti some of the sharpest criticism of his work. However, the constancy and repetition seem to be inevitable, since the author clings to an unswerving vision of the world. With this in mind, I should like to trace the concept of plot in Onetti, focusing on his most representative and outstanding protagonists, Eladio Linacero, Juan María Brausen, and Junta Larsen.

In treating his creative activity as a dream and in endowing his protagonist with the same capacity of fantasizing as his own, a writer defines the boundaries of his fictional realm and limits the scope of his work to the sphere of the oneiric and, consequently, is bound to the worlds of the abstract and the cerebral. For dreams and elaboration of fantasies pertain to man's intangible psyche, communicable only through the medium of the *logos* or abstract articulation. It is to be expected, then, that the protagonist of such a work should possess the intellectual capacity to live up to the task his author has set before him. As already stated, Juan Carlos Onetti is such a writer, and Linacero is an intellectual hero who has to confront the irreparable fate and human condition which characterizes the pathetic protagonists of the twentieth century in their "tragic impasse."[8] In his cerebral nature, Linacero is also akin to the characters which populate the urban fiction of the River Plate region.

In trying to follow the development of plot of a work like *El pozo* the reader is also bound to the confines of the mind and intellect of the protagonist, for it is within these boundaries that the transmutations of character take place. The difficulties of such a task under these circumstances are obvious. The reader has no tangible means of assessing change within the situation, actions, and fortune of the protagonist since all of these conditions are not given to the reader by the author but, rather, are reflected in the mind and consciousness of the protagonist-narrator. The only recourse we have of assessing plot development and narrative structure is through the intellect and psychological convolutions of the hero's mind, because all processes of change which constitute the plot are funneled through the thoughts of the character. Any plot evolution can only be determined at the level of the abstract. The reader, therefore, has no way by which to verify whether a transformation in situation or action has actually occurred. Instead, he must be satisfied with what repercussions a change might have on the character's psyche. As readers, we must forego the necessity to verify a completed process of change in such a case, because circumstances around a character could very well be fantasies of the protagonist as much as actualities. Once a reader undertakes to follow the work's unfolding, he must become all-accepting. The protagonist, on the other hand, is not bound by any limitations, and his psychological fate may take on any form and direction. Most true to this fact is the case of modern psychological novels, like Onetti's *La vida breve* and *El astillero,* in which a psychotic and schizoid strain in the characters psyche is not entirely absent. The traditional notion that the completion of a plot is as much dependent on the reader (insofar as expectations are aroused in him which must be attended to by the author, either by their fulfillment or by a surprising change which resolves the suspense in an unexpected way) as it is on the author no longer remains true. In the subjective novel, that is to say, in the works which are comprised of the author's and protagonist's refracted and multiplied dreams and psychic abstractions, all is a surprise or, more accurately, nothing should be surprising.

The mainstay of *El pozo*'s plot is precisely this phenomenon of psychological shift from one line of narrative to another. Thus the

reader is put on one track which the protagonist's flow of consciousness soon abandons, constantly creating a discrepancy between expectations of the reader, goals of the protagonist, and
realization or fulfillment of these. This is not to say, however, that
the author has lost control over his narrative. The phenomenon is a
methodology, a technique on Onetti's part which creates a consistency between form and metaphysical intent, just as the intentional use of an intellectual hero serves the author most efficiently
in putting forth a philosophical stance. As is the case with *Para una
tumba sin nombre,* the episodic fragmentation and disjointed series
of events have their intentionality, and, as Jaime Concha accurately
observes with respect to *El pozo's* scheme: "Its principle lies in the
lack of concurrence between what is announced and what is realized within the series; but this unfaithfulness and outlined project,
in itself expressive of an unstable will, is methodically regulated."[9]
The discrepancy within the scheme of *El pozo* is not simply the inconsistency between the protagonist's stated purpose and the failure
of its achievement in the end. It consists rather of a series of discrepancies within the narrative which result from the protagonist's
free associations, evoked within his mind by events and circumstances which emanate from psychological recesses, exposing
remote and near thoughts, indifferently and with no apparent connection. The narrative structure then becomes a series of revealed
"time pockets" embedded within the character's being. Their
revelations, seemingly indiscriminate, have an order which is closely
controlled by the author. We might call these evocations sporadic,
disjointed, and unified only by the presence of the consciousness to
which they happen. These shifts or veerings are in direct correlation
(in concurrence) with character changes that in their totality form
that "completed process of change" we call plot. Thus, the psychological free associations would represent a progression toward
the completion of an end, which might be the metamorphosis of the
protagonist from what he is at the opening of the novel to what he
becomes by the end of it. In other words, his progression represents
stages within the formation of the work.

I wish to stress emphatically at this point that the progression
which completes the plot of *El pozo,* besides not being consistent, is
circular rather than linear. The transmutations and process of completed change which determine the plot have already occurred and
are a *fait accompli* at the beginning of the work. In other words, the
protagonist is already at the very beginning what the events and

situations of the novel are to make of him. Thus, the plot may be said to be circular, for what we have between the first page and the last page of the novel is an exposition of the process by which the hero has come to be what he is. This, of course, is the author's reason for giving the work an autobiographical form.

The plot of *El pozo* is a character plot since "the synthesizing principle" of change within the novel is the character of the protagonist. Although capriciously derived through a series of psychological inconsistencies, as I have pointed out above, we see the fulfillment of the protagonist's potential. The moral character he comes to possess is foreshadowed by the events of his adolescence which he describes in retrospect within the context of the dream of "the log cabin." Linacero's thoughts, in their disjointed disarray which reveal his character, speak of an alienated man, individuated and estranged from other men and women to the point that the rest of humanity serves only to confirm his alienation and to individuate him even further. This extreme alienation is the metaphysical crux of the plot's argument, and this phenomenon fully demonstrates the shifting narrative structure and the internal discrepancies arising from the psychological state of the protagonist and his role as narrator. In their flow as a series, the psychological discrepancies give the progressive stages of the plot's formation.

Early in the novel, Linacero admits the futility of human communication to which he feels condemned. After confessing his intimate fantasy and the distant events of twenty-five-years ago, Linacero tells us that, "Only twice did I speak of the adventures with some one" (*oc*, 57). He admits to the calamitous disappointment at these attempts. Then, by enumerating, "Cordes first and later that woman of the International" (*oc*, 58), Linacero sets before us an objective order of his story of misunderstandings with humanity which have determined his character and thoughts and which convince him of the impossibility of human communion. But as soon as he prepares the reader to expect the story behind his feelings of misanthropy and estrangement, his thoughts wander back to the dream of the log cabin. He explains to the reader at this point that the eroticism of his dream is one in a myriad of literary examples. Then he remembers the occasion when he and the prostitute Hanka overheard a quarrel between two disaffected lovers, and his explanation also leads us to believe that it might have been an argument between a whore and her pimp. Subsequently, he dwells on his passionless entanglement with Hanka and

his boredom with her presence. Finally, he abandons his narration
and becomes reflective. In his thoughts he returns to what he had
set forth to narrate two pages before: "Why was I speaking of comprehension a few lines back? None of these beasts can comprehend
anything" (*oc*, 60). After this section, he takes up the narrative
thread. However, he does not follow the actual sequence of events
but begins with "that woman of the International." He is not to
mention Cordes again until the end of the novel. While we are told
of the circumstances which led to miscomprehension with Esther
(the "woman of the International"), Linacero's thoughts wander to
his relationship with his wife, whom he is indifferently divorcing,
and, finally, his free associations lead him to a discourse on the
nature of woman.

The narrative shifts enumerated above are outside of the scope of
the story the protagonist-narrator has set out to tell. They are external to the hard and fast events which proved to him the futility of
human communication and understanding. Yet, the reader realizes,
and the author well knows, that they are not extraneous to the story
and Eladio Linacero and therefore to the plot of *El pozo*. These psychological and mental meanderings represent the author's
dramatization of the progressive process of desolidarization, alienation, and individuation which the protagonist has undergone in
order to become the absurd existential figure that he is. Furthermore, these digressions give the work a symphonic quality of
rhythmic approximation and withdrawal from the skeletal structure
of the narrative. Jaime Concha has aptly called this effect, "the
musicalization of the novel" ("la musicalización de la novela") and
concludes that "the form of composition is less architectural than
musical, it is rhythm more than sculpting."[10]

There are two stories and two authors to the plot of *El pozo*.
Linacero is both the Hamlet who watches a dramatic performance
of his own play and Quixote, who has read his own story. He is not
excluded by Onetti from the activity of artistic creation, since he
"coauthors" the work. It is imperative that the "hero" of such a
novel be an intellectual capable of introspection and self-
reflectiveness. For the intellectual hero, as I already have attempted
to point out, inherently holds within his being his own alienation.
His urgent need to reflect on his existence and to reach a self-
identity creates an open clash with his desire to remain separate
from the self and be conscious of it, thus alienating himself from his
own essence. In the words of Victor Brombert, "The other tempta-

tion of the intellectual is that of self-indulgent soul-searchings which constitute another, and subtler, form of desolidarization. For narcissism, even of a cerebral type, is a way of reducing the other to the role of mirror, a way of negating the very witness."[11]

The plot of *El pozo* is plainly a character plot, since the moral and philosophical character of the protagonist comprises the essence of the work. The traditional critical concepts, however, fall short of truly defining the nature of a plot in a work like *El pozo*. There really is no fundamental change either in the thought or in the moral character of the protagonist. There is only a fruition and a fulfillment of the potential the hero manifests from the very beginning of his existence. The novel and its events function to confirm what the hero has been all along. We should keep in mind that the separateness and alienation which have come to pervade Linacero's existence were already rampant in his childhood and adolescence. The self-deprecation which dominates his life extends back to his earliest years: "As a child, I was an imbecile" ("Como niño era un imbécil") (*oc*, 50). Even before the decisive event in his life which revealed to him the unbreachable gap between the self and the other, his being and the rest of humanity, Linacero entertained an ominous anticipation. He believed with certainty that what was to result from his overt attempt at human contact was unavoidable. He also accepted as inevitable the fact that others only serve to reinforce one's alienation and to become accomplices in self-judgment, abnegation, and self-condemnation to absurdity. Thus, in relating the episode of twenty-five years ago with Ana María, Linacero tells us: "It might seem like a lie, but I remember perfectly that from the moment I recognized Ana María—from the way she carried one arm away from her body and the bending of her head—I knew everything that was going to happen that night. Everything except the end, although I was expecting something of that nature" *oc*, 52). Viewing the event in retrospect even before its actual occurrence, the protagonist sees its outcome with futile resignation when on the same page he continues to explain the occasion by stating that "the whole thing was about something that had already happened to us and its recurrence was inevitable."

We cannot truly call such a plot one of resignation since the protagonist is already resigned prior to the life he is to lead within the scope of the narrative. All we can say of this work is that its plot is already predetermined as is the condition of its protagonist who, during the course of the novel, takes an active part in the comple-

tion of the inevitable fate which awaits him, conscious all along of
its certainty and of his role as an accomplice hastening his own
doom. The protagonist, therefore, is his own antagonist, and as such
he should be considered as an "antihero" in the long line of
alienated protagonists that abound in contemporary fiction.

The legitimate successor, as Rodríguez-Monegal puts it, to Eladio
Linacero is Juan María Brausen. *La vida breve*, though an infinitely
more hermetic work than *El pozo*, in terms of plot is more accessible
from the traditional concept of the term. The plot of this key work is
comprised of splinters, scraps which correspond to the fragmented
personality of the schizoid protagonist.

III   *The Redoubling Plot*

As with *El pozo*, the transmutations within *La vida breve* are
cerebral, abstract, and psychological rather than external. All motion, change, and metamorphosis, thus have a simultaneous nature.
We cannot fruitfully attempt to trace through a linear progression
the metastasis of Brausen-Arce-Díaz Grey within the psychic personality of the protagonist. For Brausen is Brausen even while he is
Arce, and he is Brausen and Arce while he is, through oneiric
abstraction, Díaz Grey. He is also all three simultaneously even
when he denies the self through the negation of one, because the
rejection of the one, if carried to its extreme, means the obliteration
of all three.

The critical reader is confronted with a more complex problem
than in *El pozo*. In the author's first work one can pursue the evolution of plot on one single plane. Regardless of how capricious, the
consciousness and its psychological convolutions are one. In the case
of *La vida breve*, however, the protagonist's psyche ectoplasmically
multiplies itself, each of its segments assuming proportions of a u-
nit, an entirety unto itself with its own oscillations. Although the
multiple lives of the work's protagonist are essentially one, in actuality the lives within the narrative flow remain multiple and function on their individual planes. The plot, then, evolves in the
manner of parallel prongs that constantly close or expand the distance between them but never truly coincide. Thus, as Emir
Rodríguez-Monegal observes with respect to the fission Brausen-
Arce: "At some point both worlds become tangential but they never
intersect; they are on different planes; different principles govern
them and the game of living cannot be the same in both."[12] To this

duplicity we must add Díaz Grey, a mask or another projection of the protagonist in which he desperately seeks his salvation. In attempting to assess the plot development of such a work as *La vida breve*, one is forced to seek and evaluate change not only within the situation ("fortune"), moral character, and thought of one personage, but within that of *three*; with cognizance, of course, that the trilogy is in essence one, and that in the long run it is its unity which forms a single work.

The opening sentence of *La vida breve* places us within the world which will consume the double of the protagonist's personality and consummate the psychological split in his life: "Mad world—the woman said once again, as if she was mocking, as if she was translating it"(*oc*, 435). From this point on, we witness a continuous deterioration of the protagonist's psyche. Concomitant with this deterioration is the gradual formation of an alter ego which will materialize when Brausen finally ventures into the adjacent apartment of Queca, thus stepping into a new world and a new self-identity.

Concurrently, beginning with a vague mention on the novel's third page ("It would not be possible for me to write the film script that Stein talked to me about as long as I could not forget the amputated breast, formless now, crushing on the operating table like a jellyfish offering itself like a cup"), the reader is given a glimpse into a third identity projected from the protagonist's creative imagination. It is a fictitious abstraction, "a dream," one might say, yet this oneiric projection has its basis in the tedious life of Brausen and, particularly, in the irrepressible revulsion (nausée) that his wife's scarred breast evokes in him. From this first mention of the third psychological personality to its eventual completion and fulfillment, the two, the repulsive scar and the film script, will be evoked together, side by side.

Thus, from the very beginning of *La vida breve*, the plot takes various directions simultaneously, much like the plots of Ts'ui Pen in Jorge Luis Borges' "The Garden of the Forking Paths." This bifurcation, furthermore, fulfills the plan announced by Eladio Linacero ten years earlier: "It could also be a plan to go on telling an 'event' and a 'dream,' " the first here represented by Brausen's transfiguration into Arce, and the second by the imagined fantasy world of Díaz Grey.

In converting himself into his own double and counterpart, Brausen is in a long line of protagonists within imaginative fiction. I shall cite only two, one from the last century and the other from our own: Nathaniel Hawthorne's Wakefield, and Luigi Pirandello's Mattia Pascal. The first is a hallucination, the product of the author's own isolation and hermeticism; the second, a personification of melodramatic tragedy within the context of twentieth-century absurdity in man's life.

As is the case of Hawthorne's novel and Pirandello's play, in Onetti's *La vida breve* a plot completes itself at the beginning of the work. The protagonist's situation and character undergo a "completed process of change" from which ensues the beginning of a new plot. Thus, when Wakefield walks out of his home and takes lodgings in a neighboring boardinghouse, he has, as he comes to realize, converted himself into the man who twenty years later will return to cross his doorstep, a new man, a ghost of his former self. When Pirandello's Mattia Pascal decides to abandon the unbearable home situation of his life and in his absence is taken for the corpse found near the town and buried, he becomes a metamorphosis of his old self. When he finally decides to return to his former life, he feigns suicide by leaving his cane and hat on a bridge in an attempt to reverse the original transformation. He is, in the end, in the face of the impossibility of such a reversal, forced to visit his own grave and put flowers by his own tomb. Similarly, Juan María Brausen becomes Juan María Arce upon entering Queca's apartment during her absence.

As Rodríguez-Monegal points out, the protagonist's transformation when he penetrates into the world until now adjacent to him is consummated by an inversion of values that hasten Brausen's metamorphosis.[13] The character plot completes itself the moment in which the protagonist has truly and effectively ingressed into the adjacent world. This occurs when Brausen attempts to make contact with Queca, at which time he is bodily thrown out by Ernesto, one of her lovers. In the violence of the moment he realizes that he has been initiated into the world of Arce. From here, a new plot begins, and it evolves simultaneously with that other plot in which the only vestiges of the former Brausen continue to dream the imaginary world of Díaz Grey. We might say that at this point a "vida breve" ("a short life") of Brausen has ended and a new one, that of Arce, begins. As Juan María Arce, he integrates himself completely into this adjacent world, conquers Queca and, like all Onettian men do at one time or another, allows himself to wallow in the cynicism and vileness of exploiting a woman and her immoral entanglements.

The protagonist, however, like Wakefield and Mattia Pascal, does not, cannot, entirely erase his memory and consciousness of the former self. This is blatantly obvious in his obsession as Arce. Having come into this new self through violence, he knows that violence is the rule of the game in this life. To truly and unquestionably fuse himself into the new world, he feels the urge to "catharsize" himself of his former self through the murder of Queca. When he discovers that the murder he planned has already been committed by Ernesto, the reality of actual violence becomes unbearable. In the face of this actuality the Arce identity dissolves, and the second plot reverts back to the original one of which Brausen is the protagonist. Thus the work has gone through a subplot, like the first, a plot of character, and has returned to resume the initial narrative structure. The dissolution of Arce back into Brausen is manifested by his decision to shelter the assassin.

The two, Brausen and Ernesto, flee together. As fugitives they reach Santa María, the world that Brausen fabricated with Díaz Grey as a primary character. This arrival point embodies the completion of another subplot, now linked to the original and primary plot whose protagonist has all along been Brausen. The "completed process of change" which constitutes this subplot has occurred within the nature of an imaginary realm, now transformed into actual dimensions of time and space. The imaginary has become real to the point of incorporating within it the existence of its creator. Brausen becomes assimilated into the world of Santa María by a simple process. In the penultimate chapter of the novel, he lies in bed staring into the void. At that point the vision of the world he has been constructing all along reaches its completion.

In the subsequent episode, Ernesto turns himself in to the Santa María authorities. Brausen follows him. As he is apprehended, he welcomes with relief and elation his passage into the dimensions of the world about which he had dreamed: "This is what I looked for from the very beginning, since the death of the man that lived with Gertrudis for five years; to be free, irresponsible toward others, to conquer myself in a true solitude"(oc, 694). Thus, Brausen has stepped into a world of his own making, an emanation of his true solitude, there to find his true liberation. By doing so, he has completed the tautology of the work in which he appears as a character. His end is a metaphor, his creation an allegory for art and the act of creation. Such a denouement is an expression, a reiteration on Onetti's part that man's creative imagination and art are his only salvation. *La vida breve*, then, acquires a new dimension in terms of plot. The work's plot is not merely a function, a technical achievement, but a metaphoric symbol in itself which gives the novel not only its narrative structure but its meaning as well.

What in *La vida breve* is a subplot and contributes to the formation of the work's narrative structure by the addition of a third dimension, is subsequently formulated by Onetti into a full-fledged plot which spans two major and various shorter works. The world of Santa María has not only its origin in *La vida breve* and in the mind of its protagonist, but the plot of its story also begins there. The protagonist, while still an ectoplasm proper of Brausen's psyche, is Díaz Grey, the middle-aged and resigned doctor. However, as this world takes on its own reality and actual geotemporal dimensions, its original hero is relegated to the role of *ficelle* or foil (as Henry James would have it), reflecting other Onettian heroes around him in the manner of an apposition. Having objectified his oneiric projection by amalgamating himself into it, Brausen turns this phantom abstraction over to his own creator Onetti. Onetti, in turn, gives Brausen a perpetual role as the originator of the new cosmos and places his statue in the central square of Santa María with the inscription "Brausen—Founder" ("Brausen—Fundador"). From here, the role of "dreaming," of elaborating the somnolent abstraction, reverts back to the master dreamer who now undertakes the continuation of the dream and of its plot begun by one of his own fantastic projections. Onetti's departure point is precisely where Brausen left off. Having now converted the creator of Santa María into a statue and his protagonist into a *ficelle*, Onetti elevates one of the incidental figures of Brausen's creation to the role of protagonist around whom the most significant elaborations of the cosmos of Santa María and its plot must evolve. This, of course, is Junta Larsen, protagonist of *El astillero* and of *Juntacadáveres*.

Although each of these two works is a totality in itself and could be read independently of the other, a discussion based upon the major work of the author needs necessarily to interrelate the two, especially with regard to the evolution of plot. *Juntacadáveres* is a sequel of *El astillero*; though unfaithful to an actual sequence which, let us say, operates within the order of Durrell's *Alexandria Quartet* or Proust's *À la recherche du temps perdu*. In this inconsistency, Onetti manifests an obvious affinity to the narrative mode of his protagonists Linacero and Brausen and to the sequential discrepancies which emanate from their psychological state.

As was the case with *El pozo* and *La vida breve*, there is no linear
progression in the development of plot in these two major works.
The events of the later novel occur prior to those of the first. Thus,
the protagonist meets his end in *El astillero* (1961) which appears
three years before *Juntacadáveres* (1964) in which Larsen is still sur-
ging forth with optimism. In addition, the last scene which Brausen
describes in his vision of Santa María corresponds to the conclusion
of *Juntacadáveres*, which in turn is the episode of five years earlier
that opens the narrative of *El astillero*. Between *La vida breve* and
the latter two works comes *Para una tumba sin nombre*, whose
narrative sequence places it after *Juntacadáveres*. In that work there
is also passing mention of "Villa Petrus," around which the events
of *El astillero* will evolve.

What actually happened with Onetti's two latest works is that the
author began writing *Juntacadáveres*. Halfway into the completion
of *Juntacadáveres* he envisioned the quietus of Larsen, at which
time he abandoned this work and dedicated himself to the writing
of *El astillero*. Only years later did he finish the incomplete novel. It
is this procedure that, in Rodríguez-Monegal's words, explains the
graver tone of *Juntacadáveres*' second part where the work's humor
becomes more bitter, more black.[14] Adhering to the necessity of establishing a reading order which corresponds to the sequence of action and events, the Uruguayan critic, in arranging Onetti's *Obras
completas*, has placed the novels not in chronological order of
publication but in an order which corresponds to the succession of
narrative events. I shall follow this ordering in my discussion.

IV   *Junta Larsen in Santa María*

Junta Larsen could be considered as Onetti's overt contribution
to the world imagined and populated by Juan María Brausen. We
see Junta for the first time, not in the bar scene of Santa María
which Brausen describes in the penultimate section of *La vida
breve*, but in his fleeting appearance in Onetti's second novel,
Tierra de nadie. He is carried into Santa María, however, by
Brausen whom he is to replace as a focal character. In that momen-
tary first appearance, Larsen is a scant typification of the *macró*,
the pimp of the Río de la Plata. In his second appearance, he is
described by Brausen as a smallish, portly, balding man whose
lower lip trembles as he breathes. He is depicted thus in the
episode which follows the decision of the Santa María authorities to

expel him and his female cargo from the town. Some fourteen years later we are given the full significance, and also the story behind that scene. Onetti offers us a complete explication with the publication of *Juntacadáveres*, a work which marks the beginning of an intricate plot and the career of Larsen as its "hero."

Juntacadáveres is the story of Larsen's founding of the ill-fated first brothel of Santa María. In itself, independently of the "saga" of Santa María, this is one of Onetti's weakest works, stylistically and in the development of plot. On the other hand, it is the work which reveals the most about the imaginary world of Santa María. This novel seems to have been written out of a different type of necessity: a compulsion on Onetti's part to focus in on a phantasmagoric cosmogony which he had divulged in fragments and glimpses but never disclosed in its totality. In this respect, *Juntacadáveres* is an indispensable work, for it establishes the links and the derivations necessary for the true understanding of all of the author's *oeuvre*.

Stylistically, as I have pointed out elsewhere, the work suffers from a cumbersome and oppressive homogeneity in the fate of its characters, as well as from the uniform manner with which they give vent to and avow their human condition. In terms of plot, *Juntacadáveres* is unique. It is the only novel of the Santa María cycle, and among the very few in the author's overall work, that develops a plot of action (to be completed in *El astillero*) rather than a plot of character. The synthesizing principle is a change not in the moral character but in the situation of the protagonist. The situation, as a matter of fact, predominates to such an extent that the protagonist and everything that happens to him almost seem to be a pretext for its disclosure and elaboration. Furthermore, the focus given to the circumstances and thoughts of other characters, to Díaz Grey and Jorge Malabia, not to mention Barthé and Marcos Bergner, detract from the role of the protagonist to such an extent that he blends into a generalized atmosphere which almost makes of him not a protagonist but another manifestation of the *ennui* and futility which pervade the situation. The story of Junta Larsen and of his enterprise to found a brothel thus seems to be a means of revealing the nature of Santa María and the character of its citizenry. The work, therefore, is not only the story of Junta Larsen and his brothel, but is also the collective story of Santa María manifested in its reactions to the founding of the brothel.

Since the author has chosen Junta and his undertaking as the

focal point of its development, however, we cannot deny that Junta
Larsen is the salient protagonist of the work. We might say, then,
that since Santa María collectively receives as much attention in the
narrative, Junta Larsen is the protagonist and Santa María his antagonist, conspiring to thwart his plans and aspirations and eventually succeeding in completing a process of change in the situation
of the "hero." Approaching *Juntacadáveres* from this vantage point
has its justification. At a certain moment in the protagonist's life his
aspirations congeal. Their fulfillment is achieved only to be top-
pled and to perish in the end. Concurrently, certain elements within
Santa María, which provide the setting, work toward the same purpose as that of the protagonist. Others, for various reasons, toward
which the author does not conceal his antipathy, work against this
objective and through a series of interactions, means, ends, and
motives bring about its demise.

When he was still a young man and in jail for some unmentioned
infraction, Junta became aware of his calling in those six months of
introspection: "At the end of the six months, he thought that he was
born to realize two perfections: a perfect woman, a perfect brothel"
(*oc*, 920). Larsen gives himself completely to this ambition and
places his life in its service. However, Larsen does not immediately
fulfill it. His life is summed up to the moment that the opportunity
for which he has waited offers itself: "He had to live while the years
passed on; and because he had to live for the moment in which he
would come upon the girl or would be able to inaugurate the
brothel, he was committed to not look at himself, to not judge, to
not know anything about the grotesque man into which he was converting himself. Had to live and because of it, he invented the
patronage of poor, old, consumed, disdained whores" (*oc*, 921).
After many years have been consumed in pursuit of this one goal,
the opportunity finally materializes in this provincial town of Santa
María. Larsen now at the ripe age of fifty is incredulous:
". . . beneath the cunning, the reticences, and the dissimulations
that advised pride and experience, he felt ready to run to the
capital, find María Bonita, and realize with her a dream that he had
never confessed to her. He was old, incredulous, sentimental;
founding the brothel now was, essentially, like getting married
posthumously; like believing in ghosts, like acting for God's sake"
(*oc*, 831). The plot, thus, has its impetus, and the protagonist his
determination.

The novel commences with the accomplishment of Larsen's objective; the plot, then, is at its climax with the beginning of the

work. Hereafter, except for the retrospective narration, begins a descent toward a denouement which carries the inevitable Onettian negativity against the human resolve and the protagonist's tenacity. We are not allowed to forget for a moment that Onetti is the author of this work. The fruition of the protagonist's expectation and of the plot's intent is dangled for a fleeting moment before our eyes only to be snatched away, and the hero's hopes sink back into the insipid and unsavory human condition which originally gave rise to the desire to transcend it. Junta Larsen accepts his fate with a feeling of inevitability, with resignation, with a renunciation whose bitterness flows inward and nourishes a pathetic indifference. After the self-righteous denizens of Santa María succeed in closing down Larsen's establishment, the protagonist turns philosophically inward. It is a self-inversion which makes all of one's past life seem like a constant machination toward the fulfillment of a failure. Deeds and acts in life blend into a totality which signifies defeat and dissolution: "But there were no longer any deeds—the small rebirths, the changes, the frustrations, the progresses, the accommodating rectifications that each real deed signifies—rather a series of reflective acts, visible from this death to the next, and imposed by the past that had just ended" (*oc*, 894). What is left for the Onettian protagonist as of this moment is the anticipation of that gloomy and dejected inward stare with which the "hero" attempts to grasp some meaning in his defeat: ". . . from now on," the narrator tells us of Junta, "he would have to evoke the passages of his concluded life in order to be able to reconstruct the story of Junta and keep calm, before the definitive death, with the assurance of having obtained a manageable interpretation. Only that way, believing that one knows what it is that dies, can a man die in peace" (*oc*, 895).

This, like all Onettian plots already discussed, represents, at the outset, a last attempt on the part of the protagonist to conquer a saving thread of optimism which will in some way justify his existence, whether it be in the actual daily world or in the world of fantasy and dreams. The plot's denouement plunges the protagonist into utter cynicism, skepticism, and defeat. From this last and futile act of hope the only thing that remains is to come to know what is left, to understand the remnants which will be taken by the all-conclusive and absolute death. Like the end of every Onettian plot, that of *Juntacadáveres* represents a Blakeian death in life for the protagonist, even for the youthful Jorge Malabia, as Díaz Grey's authoritative assertions attest.

It is natural, therefore, that the plot of *El astillero*, Onetti's next work in the sequence of narrative action, should resolve itself in an absolute and definitive death, especially when the protagonist is the very same Junta Larsen. Having descended to a nadir as a result of the events of five years earlier which culminated in the failure of his life-long project to found a brothel, Junta returns to Santa María. Superficially, *El astillero* is the story of Junta Larsen's return to Santa María and his engagement as manager of the decaying shipyard of Petrus. The true story and its plot, however, are something else. It is here that a rigorous critical concept of *plot* becomes essential. The plot of *El astillero* is an action plot. It commences where *Juntacadáveres* left off. What we witness are the transmutations and the evolution of Junta Larsen's situation, the ensuing thoughts and feelings and the precipitated circumstances. The gist of this development is announced in *Juntacadáveres*, and, the plot is thus outlined and formulated in that work. After the decisive blow, spelled by the abortion of Junta's lifetime plans and aspirations, Onetti tells us that the only thing left for Junta is to reconstruct the pieces, the history of defeat and renunciation, so that he may arrive at some admissible meaning and manageable interpretation and give himself up to his final end. This constitutes the inner story of *El astillero* and forms its plot. Emir Rodríguez-Monegal sums it up as follows: "The real story is within and is made up of silences and pauses, the hiatus of that superficial story. It is the adventure of a solitary consciousness that returns to the past, to a world in which it was sordidly happy and was also humiliated, in search of its own lost traces, of a salvation which was also lost, of a final meaning to a meaningless life."[15]

The most crucial element in the formation of *El astillero*'s plot is the linguistic and narrative style. Here Onetti's language and technique are at their apex. The manner in which style contributes to the plot consists of the capacity of the narrator to articulate moments of stillness and silence which echo the protagonist's repeated realizations that the absolute inevitability is constantly approaching. Thus, as Rodríguez-Monegal's statement indicates, the plot of the work is within these moments of silence and hallucinatory illuminations.

These illuminations, which fill the chilling and silent moments of stillness, by their nature have a posthumous quality. The work's plot is already inevitable as it is; this haunted aura, however, raises the plot's inevitability to an even greater degree of inexorableness. The narrative structure, then, possesses an aura analogous to the

narrative of works like *Memorias póstumas de Braz Cubas* of
Machado de Assis and *La muerte de Artemio Cruz* of Carlos
Fuentes. Junta Larsen's reflections, and also the realizations attributed to him by the narrator, have the same type of retrospective
(but not conclusively past) quality as those of Artemio Cruz, who
has taken a step out of the flow of life and, as if in the middle of the
River Styx, looks back at what is left behind. We read about Junta:
"He could see himself, by seconds, in a unique locus of time; at an
age, in a place, with a past. It was as if he had just died, as if the rest
could not be anything but memory, experience, cunning, ghastly
curiosity" (*oc*, 1085). What this unique locus in time reveals to
Larsen is a view of himself, a view whose poignance and intensity
are made most extreme by the acuteness Junta Larsen's vision and
consciousness have come to acquire. Thus, he looks at himself:
"Then he thought: This body; the legs, the arms, the genitals, the
guts, what allows me a friendship with people and things; the head
that is I and for that reason does not exist for me; but there is the
cavity of the thorax, that is no longer a cavity, full of remains, wood
shavings, filings, dust, the undoing of all that mattered to me,
everything which I permitted to make me happy or miserable in the
other world'" (*oc*, 1032). Junta Larsen's words, the words of a
death mask, speak of a metempsychosis, his very own transmigra-
tion from a past self to a new one. The new self, however, is even
more ephemeral than the former; it now is a true ghost. Its evanescent transience is proclaimed by Junta's constant leave-taking. The
entire plot may be considered a continual and unremitting farewell,
a parting from the memory of a past evoked by the series of announced departures from the phantasmagoric world of the present.
The finality of death is the essence of the protagonist's obsession
and the plot's crux and content.

On one of his trips to Santa María from the shipyard, Larsen sells
a precious brooch, a gift from some unremembered woman of the
past, harboring an intuitive sensation that the sale represents a bad
omen. With the money he buys two powder boxes, one of which he
gives to Petrus' demented daughter, the other to Gálvez' woman.
With each gift Larsen repeats the same phrase: "So that you may
remember me" ("Para que me recuerde"). Women have comprised
the entirety of his life, and Junta could never help having a tinge of
pride ("un desvaído orgullo") at having touched a woman's sensitivity in some way or conquered her, even though it has come to be
second nature ("un rito indispensable"). However, this feeling has

left him, as we are told, "Not now; now there was no room for pride
or shame, he was empty, separated from his memory" (*oc*, 1089).
Conquest of women, his lifetime obsession, no longer makes any
sense or holds any promise for him. Thus, after bestowing the second gift to Gálvez' woman, Larsen simply feels "for the second time
in the night the feeling of a complex and useless triumph." Not only
Larsen himself, but also the staunch Díaz Grey is present to witness
and confirm Junta's departure with no return. "It occurs to me," he
tells us in their last meeting, "that I won't see him again" (*oc*,
1118).

This constant departure and leave-taking reduce Larsen to the
depths of irreparable solitude where man stands alone with his inconsolable human condition. "Larsen passed from nothingness to
solitude that could no longer be ameliorated by men or by deeds"
(*oc*, 1171). As the protagonist's feeling of isolation deepens,
however, his lucidity takes on a more intense, a more torturous
acuteness until, unpredictably, "The moment comes when
something of no importance or meaning obliges us to awaken and
look at things as they are" (*oc*, 1163). In such an unpredictable moment, Junta Larsen reveals a tragic vision of man and of his world.
Speaking as much of Junta as of the author, the narrator gives us a
summation: "He suddenly suspected what everyone sooner or later
comes to comprehend: that he was the only man alive in a world oc-
cupied by ghosts, that communication was impossible and not even
desirable, that pity was as good as hate, that a tolerable loathing, a
participation between respect and sensuality was the only thing that
could be demanded of anyone and that anyone should impart" (*oc*,
1124).

It is also in one of a series of such revealing moments in which
Junta Larsen begins to feel the approaching of his death and
accepts it with the same resigned attitude as he accepts everything
else. While feigning, disinterestedly, his position behind a desk in
Petrus' shipyard, he feels, he intuits his end "like a sick man can
know; he recognized all of the external symptoms but put much
more stock in the message his own body was giving him, in the
meaning of boredom and ennui" (*oc*, 1168 - 69). Just as unevent-
fully, we are told that one rainy night as he seeks the moon in the
sky to find only its metallic glow: "It was then that he accepted
without objections the conviction of being dead" (*oc*, 1192). From
here on Junta Larsen is totally unconcerned about his past or his
present. In his final night in the rusted shipyard, he is neither past

nor present: "In that hour, in that circumstance, he no longer was Larsen or anybody" (*oc*, 1199). He is running acceptingly toward the void, "trying not to be, to convert his solitude into absence." The flight is made more desperate when he hears and sees in that night the bleeding body of Gálvez' woman giving birth, generating a new life which will begin the futile and desperate cycle anew. In his despair, Junta Larsen, symbolically, like Quentin breaking his watch at the beginning of *The Sound and the Fury*, attempts to halt time; he turns in his timepiece in compensation for being carried off by the boatmen, thus, allegorically, giving up his time. The boatmen carry him off, in one version to parts unknown, and in an alternate version to his death.

Junta Larsen's particular death epitomizes Onetti's aesthetics as well as his metaphysics. There is at the end of what criticism generally accepts as Onetti's masterpiece a convergence of these two aspects of the author's work. Metaphysically, *El astillero*'s conclusion is a tautology of the novelist's pessimism and omnipresent feeling of futility. Aesthetically, the work ends on a note of ambiguity so typically Onettian and, as always, manages to aggravate even further man's helplessness in the face of his inexorable fate

CHAPTER 6

Full Circle: The Cosmic Self-betrayal

IN November, 1973, Onetti published his latest work, *La muerte y la niña (Death and the girl)*. A few months later, the major part of one of the first novels the author wrote (*Tiempo de abrazar*) appeared in a volume along with his little known, early short stories. The coincidence of the two publications which came within three months of each other is meaningful: a cycle begun in the early 1930s is closing in upon itself some forty years later. In the foregoing pages of this study I have attempted to trace the principal course of Onetti's literary project. Now, I would like to examine the peculiar convergence of its starting point, and (as of this moment) its peroration.

It would appear that the Onettian world is condemned to abandon its own reality infinitely. The men and women who populate this mythical cosmos of literature are also damned by an inescapable necessity to abdicate forever to a new plane of "reality" or "unreality" from which, in turn, they have to avenge themselves through constant eschewal.

La muerte y la niña stands as the latest reminder of this fate to which all Onettian personages, and the author himself seem to be perpetually predestined. I include the author in the coterie since this work, like many of the novels and stories which came before it, is self-reflective: a type of Chinese box which frames a story within a story thus elucidating its own making while at the same time, it serves the author and his character as a vehicle for venting their fatality and irremediable destiny. In this respect, *La muerte y la niña* partakes of the basic principles which went into the making of works like *Para una tumba sin nombre* and *La vida breve*.

The basic problem posited by this new novel is the same as that which set Onetti on a career as novelist: the problem of time and its corrosive machinations, the corruption of innocence and the ensuing degradation to which humanity and the human spirit become

126

subjected. In the recovered fragments of *Tiempo de abrazar* the confrontation with the demoralizing and desecrating forces of experience is embodied by Jason, the protagonist of the fragments, and Virginia Cras, the symbol of purity and incarnation of his youthful ideals. The story of the work is essentially that of Jason's struggle against the contamination of his own ideals and of the "virgin" spirit, the object of his love. The protagonist titters on the floundering edge of this dialectic. Through his compulsive precognition of youth's fall from grace, however, he is, in a way, already demoralized. His obsessive preoccupation with the process has rendered him thus, although he does not achieve, at least within the limited scope of the work's fragments, the gnawing cynicism which marks the matured Onettian heroes. The published fragments consist of the novel's first twelve chapters, two of which (Chapters 6 and 7) had appeared in *Marcha*, the Uruguayan weekly, in 1943, as well as Chapter 19 which also appeared that same year as a fragment in the same publication.

The work begins with this dialectic of purity and corruption by counterposing Jason with his aging professor of French literature, M. Gigord. The latter, self-involved and impressed by his own rhetoric, decrepit physically as are the banal generalities in which he speaks, provokes a sadness, an inexplicable disgust in Jason which is almost physical: "Sad and disgusted; infinitely sad and disgusted. . . . A column of filthy smoke was going from his stomach to his brain."[1] As he watches M. Gigord's taxing ascent up the stairs, he cannot help but speculate on a similar fate which awaits him within a matter of half a century. Provoked by a perverse desire of self-denigration, he finds himself "perversely searching the most painful image, the most humiliating and ridiculous. The poor, pitiful and contemptible thing that his brain would become; the residue of man into which he would be transformed" (*T*, 148).

Jason tries to decipher the ties which unite him to M. Gigord as a fellow human but discovers that their only likeness lies in the animal functions of life. He suddenly comes to the realization, an awareness which will definitively set him and all Onettian protagonists apart from humanity, that the world is replete with the likes of M. Gigord, that they rule the world: "he thought that thousands of M. Gigords surrounded him daily in the office, at the beaches, in the streets, in the tramways. And they needed not be old; they were all born with a tired imagination, infinitely mediocre, ridiculous, and brutal" (*T*, 153). Jason feels a pathetic

abhorrence toward the decrepit man and thinks of how easy it
would be to strangle him right there, in the solitude of the corridor.
He finds the idea revolting however, "by merely imagining his
fingers on the ruddy skin of the neck" (*T*, 153). Jason's revulsion in
the face of man as object, his alienation born of an antagonistic
counterpose between himself and the rest of the world, bespeak the
existential feelings of many Onettian characters, the most obvious
being Eladio Linacero and Juan María Brausen. The first is contem-
poraneous to Jason, since we know that Onetti wrote a first version
of *El pozo* during the time in which he must have been composing
Tiempo de abrazar. The striking similarity between the two works
is, therefore, not at all surprising.

Chapters 2 and 3 of *Tiempo de abrazar* are basically variations on
the theme of human decadence and degeneration. The second
chapter focuses on the material, man's usury as the agent of his corruption, while the third consists of a disjointed intellectual discussion among the contemporaries of Jason who provoke an equally
repulsive emotion within him. Their statements are as hollow and
hypocritical as the spent and puerile affirmations of M. Gigord. It is
here that Jason becomes acquainted with Virginia Cras. While the
others carry on their paltry, intellectual repartee, Jason lives in a
world of private impressions, images, and fantasy. He is engaged in
a silent dialogue with himself: "When a man's inner life does not
harmonize with the external life, with what is surrounding him,
there is nothing to do. Shut up and be off. That is the great wisdom,
Mr. Jason" (*T*, 161). This chapter represents the pivotal point of
Tiempo de abrazar. While it focuses on Jason's alienation, it also
brings together the protagonist with Virginia. The remaining ten
chapter-fragments evolve around the circumstances elaborated in
the first part of the novel.

While time emerges as the antagonist to man's innocence and
human dignity, sexuality appears to be the downfall of women, the
inevitable force that pushes girls into womanhood which for Onetti
becomes analogous to conformity, fraud, and sordidness. Thus,
while Jason is in the process of falling in love with Virginia Cras and
her purity, the thought of her sexuality and womanhood does not
spare him the assault upon his sentiments and thoughts of innocence. "Virginia's profile was pure, infantile, sweet with innocence. That expression bothered him. How could she have that
gentle gesture of candor and at the same time a body of a woman?
Could he forget by any chance that her sex rested on the soft leather

of the seat? She had a sex and. . . . He shuddered with anger; she had a sex and pretended not to know it, sustaining a hypocritical gesture of purity" (*T*, 164). Time and sexuality are a certainty. The passage into conformity and desecration become, therefore, inevitabilities. In the face of this certainty, Onetti's men, as I have endeavored to point out in the preceding pages of this study, recoil into evasion and resort to flight only to discover that their newly attained haven holds the same fate as the one they eluded. The end result, if there is an end, is the malaise, the pathos, the self-indulgent rhetoric which constitutes the paramount cynicism of *La muerte y la niña*. The element of self-righteousness possesses a convincing strength in the biliousness of Onetti's alienated heroes. Thus, they seek to avenge not only their fate but also the destiny of the women in their world. The most common method for this "vindication" appears to be the male protagonist's humiliating assault on womanhood and female sexuality at the physical as well as the abstract, spiritual plane, not to mention the social and economic planes. Let me take each of these recourses of evasion and the humiliation of the feminine in turn.

The evasion occasioned by the nausea and disgust provoked by a corrupt and contaminating reality initiates the elaborate, farcical and mythopoeic process of a vicious cycle which will spell an all-embracing paralysis of the Onettian world. The makings of the entire process has its beginnings in these very first fragments of Onetti's writing, and in those first stories which were written and published during those same years of the early 1930s. Since the same elements constitute the short stories and the more extensive novels and novellas, I shall, once again, focus primarily upon the latter.

In the fourth chapter of *Tiempo de abrazar*, we witness for the first time the escapist instinct of the Onettian hero attempting to elude the "here and now" for a refuge in the preferred time and place of illusions and imaginary geographies. In this chapter Jason is reunited with Cristina, his lover with whom he is falling out of love. At the heart of this disengagement, as the work explicitly indicates in its eleventh chapter, are Cristina's and Virginia's peculiar ways of *being* women: Cristina is sexually aggressive, her body, movements, and words are her arms. Virginia, "the young girl" ("la muchachita"), on the other hand, is more subtle, not as direct; she attracts not with the laughter of womanhood but with her silence (*T*, 224 - 25). While he still has to cope with the reality of Cristina's womanhood, however, Jason malingers in a state of fantasy which carries him far away to less noxious lands: "Life was useless and painful; but an indolence of the Sea of the Antilles—palms, huts, white uniforms kept him indifferent and calm in the chair, his legs stretched over the table" (*T*, 175).

In the chapter which follows, Jason once again lapses into the tropical dream world of fantasies as he finds himself incapable of communicating his feelings to Virginia (*T*, 190 - 91). The most obvious flight from reality (and the most fecund fantasies for works to come), however, surface in Chapter 6 which appeared as an independent fragment with the title of "Excursión."[2] The events of this part of the work are comprised of a literal flight of Jason to the countryside. It becomes apparent, however, that the protagonist is deserting human urbanity and its abhorring civilization more than embracing the countryside and its settlements. Jason's, and I suspect Onetti's, understanding of the country emerges as the view of the Sunday city motorist who takes his occasional excursion beyond the city limits but is still in view of the sprawling metropolis. The fundamental problem for the hero, as well as for his author, is the city, its multitude, and their individuated, existential circumstance: "Perhaps the city was the cause of his unhappiness. A small escape, a few hours of forgetting the business establishments, the hurried men of the streets, the music of the cafés, the multitudes of spectacles" (*T*, 192). As he approaches the provincial railway town, Jason realizes that it really was not what he looked for ("Pero no era allí donde quería ir"). Walking down the country road he hears a voice singing of a distant mountain and realizes that it is there, the distant mountain of the song that he yearns (*T*, 193). Jason's idyllic and impossible refuge is a foreshadowing of Eladio Linacero's "log cabin" in the snowy Klondike of Alaska and of Aránzuru's utopian, illusion island of Faruru, not to mention Juan María Brausen's Santa María.

All of these multiple and multitudinous worlds of evasion, including Jason's, are foreshadowed in the first story Onetti ever published when he was twenty-four-years old and was living his first stint in Buenos Aires. "Avenida de Mayo—Diagonal—Avenida de Mayo" appeared in *La Prensa* on the first day of 1933. It was selected by this publication as one of the ten best short stories. One could affirm justifiably that this story, the story of a man walking down Florida Street of Buenos Aires, mixing his stream of consciousness-hallucinations with the images and headlines which bombard any urban dweller on a busy thoroughfare, is Onetti's entire literary *oeuvre* in a germinal, encapsulized form. Like Jason, Eladio Linacero, Aránzuru, Brausen, Junta Larsen, and Díaz Grey, the story's protagonist, Victor Suaid, is trapped in the life-stream of a world noxious to him and in which he would rather not be. Like all of the Onettian characters named here, Suaid tries to escape to an imaginary life, a geography of his fantasy, and seeks an identity of his own invention. His most notable chimera is a polar geography, Alaska, the Yukon, and Jack London, the life of strength and action of the lumberjacks and the mounted police. When *El pozo* is published six years later, we see a similar visionary geography in the Alaskan winter snows which purify Eladio Linacero's drab existence in a city garret.

Three years later, with the short story "El posible Baldi," Juan Carlos Onetti elaborates an explicit instance of a character assuming an identity and personal history totally alien to his objective reality but obviously very much a part of his psychic fantasies. It will be some fourteen years later with the appearance of *La vida breve* that Baldi will "reemerge" as Juan María Brausen and "the possible Brausen" who will assume the name of Arce as well as the many "short lives" of his imagination. In the short story of 1936 Baldi is an unshaven, vagrant city dweller who walks along with his hat cocked toward the back of his head, with his hands in his pockets. He finds a type of "courage" in the routine of the day which alleviates the tedium of confronting the passing of time, "Secure in the face of the problem of the night, already resolved by the barbershop, dinner, and the movies with Nené." This same Nené will return to occupy a principal role in the novel *Tierra de nadie* which is to follow the story some five years later. Like all the individuated protagonists of Onetti's literature, Baldi manifests a dreaded fear of the night, its solitude, and the tedium of the imperceptible passage of the night hours which have the capacity to cloister and alienate in a claustrophobia of penumbra, heat, sounds, and memory. For the moment, however, "the problem of the night" is resolved, and Baldi finds the confidence and acceleration to conjure a life of adventure and conquest. He depicts himself as a run-away Negro hunter in the diamond mines of the South African Transvaal. He convinces the credulous, young streetwalker he has engaged in conversation of this "possible Baldi" and by doing so he convinces himself: "until the other Baldi was so alive that he could think of him as an acquaintance" (*T*, 26).

However, Baldi falls into the inevitable trap of all Onettian apostates which turns the self-engendered farce into a ruthless mechanism of *ennui* and self-flagellation: the comparison and contrast between actuality and fantasy. The inner dialectic at that moment becomes stronger than either "reality," actual or imagined, and the protagonist is transformed into the battlefield of a Bovaristic struggle: "And then, suddenly, an idea pierced him tenaciously. A thought plunged him into affliction. . . . He compared Baldi the lie with himself, with this calm and harmless man that was telling stories to the Bovarys of the Plaza Congreso. With the Baldi who had a girl friend, law studies, the respectful smile of a porter. . . . A slow, idiotic life, like the whole world" (*T*, 27). The protagonist's thoughts yield to resigned explanations of his respectability, to regret, and self-justification: "Because Dr. Baldi was not capable of jumping on the deck of a ship, laden with sacks or wood. Because he was not up to accepting that life is something else, that life is what cannot be made in the company of loyal women, nor sensible men. Because he had closed his eyes and surrendered, like everyone. Employees, gentlemen, office managers" (*T*, 27).

The process of escapist fantasy, its painful comparison with the inescapable actuality, and resigned contrition does not end here. The Onettian hero turns outward at this point to assail those human beings who have knowingly or not provoked the imaginary, possible self and thus indirectly produced that painful and repentant dialectic between fantasy and actuality. Thus, with this early story we witness the protagonist directing his resentment against women (the only human beings from whom the Onettian hero expects an understanding of his impasse, but also whom he holds responsible, in the final analysis, for his inevitable contrition). Baldi, then, is the first in a long line of defrauded farceurs who feel the compulsive need to denigrate the women who gullibly share in their farce. As he is about to part, Baldi hands the woman a large bill, a payoff for having partaken of the evasive fantasies, "feeling that he hated her, that he would have given anything not to have found her." Before the woman's perplexity Baldi "spoke with a somber face, making the words sound like insults" (*T*, 27). He tells the confused woman: "I earn that money which I give you, pushing cocaine. In the North." The indomitable farceur thus invents another "possible life" for himself which is abusive to his commonplace respectability and, at the same time, insulting to the woman's dignity.

It would appear that the most provocative element found by Onetti's heroes in women is their own escapist Bovarism which they project upon them, and whom they then proceed to chastise and humiliate. Thus, in more ways than one, Onettian women become scapegoats and the object of the heroes virulent outlet. Baldi's manner of subjecting the particular woman of the story to this humiliation is only one of the ways in which this rancorous, wry reprisal is accomplished by Onetti's discontented, male protagonists. A sexual involvement which results in serving the same purpose is not uncommon, and we witness its beginnings also with these first writings.

As I have mentioned previously, woman's sexuality proves to be her perdition in the Onettian cosmos. Accordingly, the men instrumental in inducing it are more acutely concerned with woman's loss of innocence than the women themselves. In fact, Onetti's women emerge as well-adjusted and august human beings in the face of their inevitable fall. It is the men who suffer a crisis and consequently impose a predicament upon the women. The case of Jason and Virginia in *Tiempo de abrazar* is exemplary. In the eighth chapter of this work Jason's obsessive preoccupation arises out of the fact that Virginia might, and will, as he intuits much to his anguish, topple from the pedestal of purity which he has created for her in his mind: "And then, if the years deformed Virginia and the fresh, uncontaminated young girl turned into an honest Miss, regretful of that error of adolescence. . ." (*T*, 208). Jason expresses his feelings to Virginia when he confesses: "I would not like you to be like all the others, a hundred percent woman, to the point of saturation. . . . . At times, even everything feminine becomes nauseating to me" (*T*, 216).

There is a perverse, puritanical strain which operates in creating an antagonistic posture between the men and the women in Onetti's fiction. Incapable of dealing with his own humanity and human needs, the Onettian hero converts his feminine counterpart into a temptress. In his mind she works toward his own fall and her own degradation. As Onetti's world matures and his protagonists come of age, this feeling will crystallize into an inalienable right which the men evoke for the purpose of exploiting women. For now, however, the antagonism in the male's psychological incapacity takes on a savage need to humiliate with a vengeance. Jason, like his fictive contemporary, Eladio Linacero of *El pozo*, finds himself

invaded by a feeling of rancor, hate, and the necessity to draw upon
himself the same sentiments from Virginia. As he stands on the
verge of kissing her "he felt a sudden hate, a savage instinctual
bestiality before the calm woman at his side, before her tranquil
voice, before her dark hand that was not retreating. He took her by
the shoulders, blind, furious" (*T*, 204).

This transformation of an amorous entanglement into sado-
masochistic punishment, as Jorge Ruffinelli points out in his
prologue, is reminiscent of Linacero's sexual assault on Ana María.
The protagonist of *El pozo* overcomes his elder cousin with a savage
fury. Enjoyment there, as in *Tiempo de abrazar*, yields to a desire to
humiliate and punish: "She was able to free an arm and she dug her
nails into my face. I then searched for the most humiliating, the
most odious caress" (*oc*, 53).

The humiliating assault on the feminine, however, in the end
proves as futile as any possibility of reconciliation with the time-
bound human condition and its inexorable conformity. As in this
latter circumstance, the Onettian protagonist is forced to seek
refuge in the imagistic impressions of fantasy and the crystallized
moments of ethereal memory: "A strange feeling of hostility toward
Virginia hardened his face. Ah, no: not even she could take away
from him the graceful image of that young girl, standing on the step
of the train that was moving away, smiling at him, looking at him,
moving the caress of her hand toward him" (*T*, 217). In the final
fragment of the work Jason and Virginia will meet again. It will not
be for the sake of a reconciliation but for a leave-taking which implies a longer, perhaps definitive separation. In this final parting the
dilemma of the Onettian hero comes to the foreground. While he
realizes that there is no hope for any meaningful human communion, either spiritual, physical, or emotional, he cannot muffle or
immolate the impending solitude, self-confrontation, and the
realization of a ubiquitous discontentment: "*He was afraid of his
impending solitude. . . . Everything was going to remain without
any sense incomprehensible like a written symbol whose key had
been lost*. And, suddenly, even more intense, the fear of prolonging
the leave-taking" (*T*, 245). And now, in that forsaken and self-
perpetrated but inevitable desert of solitude, Jason commences not
only his homelessness, but the malingering career of all Onettian
heroes who will span the duration of a fictitious cosmogony. Alone
with the illusory reality of imagination and an inconsolable
memory, Jason outlines the plan: "Now, everyday, a war of

cleverness or courage, against everyone, in order to conserve and defend her. He stood up with a hardened face and began to walk around. To fight against all; against the immense human stupidity, against the cowardice of the human beast" (*T*, 246).

The background supplied by these early works are crucial to the Onettian cosmogony in more ways than one. As I have tried to elaborate in the chapter of this study which deals with the author's modes of characterization, the Onettian protagonists are presented as complete manifestations of an immediate present whose fixed past remains in the shadows. With each important character we are given a final culmination without any of the particular lineaments or their evolution as they combined to form the personage confronting the reader of a given work. We know nothing of Junta Larsen's early, formative years, for example. We are equally ignorant of Juan María Brausen's past as we are of Díaz Grey's. Insofar as Onetti's heroes embody characteristics of a generic personality which one could call the Onettian Man, the travails and preoccupations of these early protagonists could be taken as the formative experiences of that personality. In this respect, it would appear that Jason's tenacious determination to conserve the pure, ethereal image of Virginia in the subjectivity of his private dreamworld has proliferated through Onetti's works to all of his protagonists. Perhaps even the most sardonic and cynical among them are in some way constructing a wall of travesty in order to protect an ineffable image and ephemeral experience which can only survive in those recesses farthest from reality. Jason's fears that upon losing Virginia everything would "remain without any sense, incomprehensible like a written symbol whose key had been lost" were realized and continue to be realized in every Onettian hero.

It would not be unreasonable to affirm, therefore, that the illusionist worlds of all these farceurs are more than illusive chimeras. I believe these "farces" are ethereal worlds in reconstruction whose *keys* to their symbols are in the firm grip of Onetti whose repeated self finds embodiment in each of his protagonists. When the repeated history of this constructive and reconstructive process converges upon itself in a concurrent simultaneity, the farce, the "illusive chimera," ascends to a denouement which we call "myth." Such a moment is clearly achieved, as I have pointed out already, in *La vida breve* where we witness the rise of a mythical world: Santa María. The denouement of this moment will be sustained for the rest of Onetti's career by the saga of that myth. Thus, Santa María

becomes more than mere allegory, for the nature of myth in Onetti
has proved to be more univocal than allegorical; that is to say, it
does not merely posit a philosophical stance but an independent,
historical reality unique to itself. Its universal quality is an incidental but inherent by-product which rises out of its own truth and
faithfulness to itself. The transcending and transcendental quality
of Onetti's myth, what makes it cosmic, is derived through a
microcosm which, as *La muerte y la niña* attests, has always
adhered to its own "truth." This unwavering constancy is, I believe,
the key to Onetti's latest novel and its defrauded reality of apostatic
degeneration. Approaching the Uruguayan author's latest work in
any terms other than as a culmination of an evasionist myth and farcical cosmogony would, I believe, leave the reader most disap-
pointed. *La muerte y la niña* stands as the ultimate in farce, but it
also bespeaks those Onettian traits which have so frequently drawn
the disapprobation and diatribes of critics: rhetoric and authorial
self-indulgence. The problem of rhetorical outbursts is complicated
by the fact that a reader not initiated into the origins of the Onettian cosmogony will find the novel's rhetoric incomprehensible,
since it is directed, for the most part, toward the antecedent
histories in the Santa Marían saga. The work then emerges as a
Nemesis, an implacable invective aimed at its own genesis.

The story of *La muerte y la niña* is comprised of various individual histories commonly linked by the art of travesty in varying
degrees of sardonic subtlety and finesse. The sentimental education
of Goerdel, the years-long process of his initiation into farce by the
grand master of farceurs, Father Bergner, emerges as the main
thread of the novel. As a new figure in the Onettian cosmogony,
Goerdel and his story are overshadowed by the overwhelming
presence of an old-time denizen, Díaz Grey. The middle-aged doctor appears here as more than a mere observer, his traditional role in
the saga of Santa María. His presence as well as his demeanor take
on a new air, a diminished distance from the story. The change is
unfortunate because it seems to have compromised Díaz Grey's independence as a character, as an authorial *ficelle* (foil); his
narrating and reflective voice has been mitigated. To be more
precise, he speaks and sounds more and more like Juan Carlos Onetti! Perhaps such a change is inevitable since, as we discover in this
work, Díaz Grey now is linked by ties stronger than ever to his companions in Santa María's ship of fools. He is wed to Angélica Inés,
Petrus' demented daughter. Petrus, the reader will recall, is the

archimposter and sublime high priest in the sham of *El astillero.*
Jorge Malabia, the sensitive adolescent of *Juntacadáveres* and the
blooming cynic of *Para una tumba sin nombre* also reappears. He
emerges as a caricature whom we only see through the wry sarcasm
of Díaz Grey's rhetoric. In this respect, Jorge Malabia best typifies
La muerte y la niña. Just as this character has evolved into a
caricature of the earlier Jorge Malabia, Onetti's novel comes across
as a parody, a hollow echo, and an ingenuous mimesis of the
author's previous works. Sadly enough, with this novel Onetti is
derisively mimicking the Onetti of a more vigorous, imaginatively
ambiguous, and creatively richer period. On its own terms as an independent work, therefore, *La muerte y la niña* is a sad disappointment. However, it does possess a saving grace which is compen-
sating to the reader who has followed the evolution of the
Uruguayan writer's *oeuvre:* its implications in terms of the
mythopoeic development and the philosophical grounds of the
Onettian cosmogony.

  In many respects the author's latest novel seals off the world of
Santa María and its myth definitively. It closes a cycle by positing a
stance which bespeaks the impossibility of transcendence beyond
farce. The game is accepted as an end in itself. Its possibilities as a
means toward a more authentic reality are terminally sundered. The
only thing which remains, therefore, is to perfect the farcical
gamesmanship and to reflect upon it in a stasis which has petrified
all chances of going beyond. All the characters in the novel, then,
place their energies in the service of their own sentence as condemned creatures, destined to gesticulate within the snare of an
oneiric, illusory stratagem. Their only hope is to perpetuate the
game of travesty and their mastery of its moves. Accordingly,
Father Bergner undertakes the education of Goerdel whom he has
adapted as a disciple at a very early age. Goerdel does well by his
master and becomes rather distinguished as a farceur. The novel
focuses on his craftsmanship which culminates in the death of the
young woman whom he appropriates along with her inheritance.
Upon her mysterious death in the pangs of child bearing, a death
whose responsibility is insinuated to rest with Goerdel, the young
initiate is led by his master toward the house of Insauberry, the
twelve-year-old daughter, and the family's millions. Needless to
say, this farce is also consummated. When we reach the narrative
present of the novel we discover that Goerdel has returned to Santa
María following a long absence abroad. He has returned with the

purpose of vindicating himself from the responsibility of his wife's death whose circumstances point an accusing finger at him. His strategy is to prove the dubiousness of his paternity in the ill-fated pregnancy. Dr. Díaz Grey and Jorge Malabia are called upon to collaborate in the exoneration.

The task that Jorge Malabia and Díaz Grey are called upon to perform is reminiscent of that earlier collaboration in another work, *Para una tumba sin nombre.* As in this earlier novel, they are faced with the problem of organizing "evidence" in order to construct another possible story or other possible stories emanating from the same set of circumstances. When Díaz Grey accepted a similar task years before, he saw it to its completion and derived the satisfaction of authorial godliness which accompanies such an achievement. He confessed then: "The only thing that counts is that when I finished writing it, I felt at peace, sure of having achieved the most important thing that could be expected from this sort of task: I had accepted a challenge, I had converted into victory at least one of the daily defeats" (*oc*, 1046). Now, a decade and a half later, Díaz Grey is no longer sure of the possibility of an independent act on his part which could give him the opportunity to partake of his creator's authorial power. With rhetorical bitterness and resignation, he arrives at the realization that any course of action on his part is merely the enactment of another's volition, a performance of Juan María Brausen's will which has given birth to Santa María, everyone in it, including Díaz Grey, and all their gestures. This realization by Díaz Grey has grave ontological implications, for it means that this middle-aged doctor has suddenly become aware of his phantomlike nature, an imaginary phantasm to the second degree, dreamed by Brausen who is in turn the brainchild of Juan Carlos Onetti. In the face of such a realization Díaz Grey reaches the inevitable consciousness that all of his acts are a compounded farce whose performance he is destined to enact as an oneiric jester in a realm of myth with a long history, albeit an elusive and illusory history. With the precognition of his own *unreality*, Díaz Grey and his entire world, Santa María, become unreal for the reader as well. The farce which more than twenty years earlier had evolved into myth suddenly turns on itself and devolves once again into farce. Díaz Grey's realization, a revelation thrust upon the reader and the cosmogony of Santa María by Onetti, tears asunder the integrity of a coherent and unified myth which had been hitherto, as Coleridge would have it, successful in "suspending our disbelief" for more than two decades. Onetti thus emerges as a Gnostic who, like the demiurges in Borges' "Circular Ruins," must experience the periodic annihilation of his cosmogonies so that he and we may not forget their ethereal construction and oneiric nature.

Although nihilistically rendered, the peroration of the Onettian myth is inherently an optimistic denouement. Periodic destruction implies periodic regeneration, and in the myth of the eternal return time and succession become secondary to motion and dynamism. In Díaz Grey's contrition this perquisite note also emerges: "That time in itself does not exist is demonstrable; it is the child of movement and if it were to cease moving we would not have time, or consummation, nor would we have beginnings or ends. In literature time is always written with a capital letter" (*T*, 31).

CHAPTER 7

Conclusion: Onetti and
the New Latin American Novel

THE technical formulation of Onetti's fiction is individualistic. The recurring consistencies in structure and narrative technique are not ends in themselves but serve as means to a vision of reality and to an attitude toward the cosmos. Nor does Onetti submit unconditionally to any reality, abstract or concrete, as his statements in the interview with María Esther Gilio (cited in the first chapter) expressively indicate. Stated in more technical terms, Onetti is neither a formalist nor is he a dogmatic objectivist affirming and glorifying reality as an aesthetic end in itself. He is not philosophically, socially, and most significant for this study, aesthetically a partisan of any given conceptual system in his approach to the art of the novel. Like Faulkner, he is a novelist simply by virtue of the fact that he writes novels, or one could say that Onetti is an aestheticist in the same way that Albert Camus is a philosopher. What prevails in both is not a set of ideas as governing principles. Rather, we witness an undeclared attitude which is not proclaimed, but which articulates itself through their work.

In a century which is overburdened with "isms" and "schools," Onetti, like Faulkner and Camus, has avoided the limited horizon of dogma in his approach to fiction and has consequently created what is already proving to be a lasting art, capable of enduring the timely and timelessness of literary modes.

Within the context of the contemporary Latin American novel, Juan Carlos Onetti has proved himself an obstinate agnostic. His unfailing ill luck, chronicled by Rodríguez-Monegal, with respect to literary prizes, attests to Onetti's skepticism toward the timely in the modes of the novel. It should be remembered, however, that Faulkner did not begin to receive his present acclaim in the United States or recognition by the Swedish Academy until nearly fifteen

years after the publication of his major works. We should also keep
in mind that Bernardo Verbitsky, who won the literary prize of the
Editorial Losada in 1941 over Onetti, has fallen into oblivion, as
have the taste and literary criteria of the jury of that time. This,
however, was only the beginning in a long series of *malentendidos*
("misunderstandings") in a career of anachronisms, as Rodríguez-
Monegal calls it. Undaunted and sustained by the profound conviction in what he had to impart, Onetti persevered in his Platine
namelessness. Often with an unmistakable skepticism which never
seems to have fallen into bitterness, he continued to create an artistic cosmos imbued with the same spirit of hope, failure, resignation, and perseverance.

Like all great works of art, Onetti's have been conceived and executed in isolation. Suspicious of the formal techniques and working
devices at his disposal, devoted to the reality of the objective world
and of the human condition, but with irreverence, Onetti has
always maintained the primacy of his vision and of its substance.
The medium has never ceased to be merely a means for Onetti. The
ends always transcend these means as well as the crude matter of
reality in his art, even when they occupy a focal attention within a
given work.

In attempting to draw some conclusions regarding Onetti's
"aesthetics" and his attitude toward the formal structure of the
novel, two key works present themselves as outstanding points of
departure. *Los adioses* and *Para una tumba sin nombre,* two of
Onetti's short novels, confront the technical devices of the novelistic
art quite openly and act as demonstrations of the art of the novel
from a theoretical as well as from a practical point of view. In addition to their transcendent philosophical problems, they are novels
about writing a novel. The author's posture toward the problem of
aesthetics, if one can take the liberty of interpreting an attitude as a
posture, in these two works emerges as a pose of suspicion, of a
profound skepticism and serious misgivings which the author har-
bors toward his own art. The two works could be taken as an undeclared, but emphatically articulate, testimonial and philosophical treatise on the character of twentieth-century aesthetics.
They point out the futility of formalism, of the capacity of technique to distort, and the potential nihilism and meaninglessness in the
move toward art for art's sake, where art ceases to have any
relevance or significance. On the other hand, they are an abnegation of crude reality and of art which affirms reality to the extent of

assigning to it absolute aesthetic value. Oddly enough, modern art has more than confirmed these possibilities. In the contemporary Latin American novel examples are not lacking for either of these two possibilities. In either instance, we derive positive moral and aesthetic values through negative art.

Onetti's misgivings about technique in the aesthetics of narration are most emphatic in *Los adioses*. The artist's formal *modus operandi* hitherto employed by the novelist is overtly brought under the sharp focus of suspicion. Art, fundamentally an exercise in selectivity and delimitation, is questioned as a valid medium of understanding totality and integral reality. The form of this challenge is, as already pointed out, a trap skillfully set for the reader. It is the first time in which the author openly confronts the problem of technique and constructs a work around this problem. In its final completed form *Los adioses* is not an affirmation but an expression of doubt and distrust of formal novelistic aesthetics. It is an open confession of the writer, achieved through the embarrassment of the reader. For the work is not only a challenge to the art of the novel, it is also Onetti's way of taking the reader to task for his gullibility, for his part as accomplice to questionable methods which convince us that things are other than they actually are. Through a double-pronged attack such as this, Onetti questions the entire spectrum of twentieth-century novelistic aesthetics at all levels of contemporary society.

Art, though at its best conceived and executed in isolation, does not function in a vacuum. Its birth and the forms which it assumes are generated by a greater magnitude of forces than the writer, who frequently finds himself in the role of agent or midwife. To this end, the sociocultural determinants which have given rise to the contemporary Latin American novel and its aesthetics are amply documented.[1] Onetti, then, writing nearly twenty years prior to today's critics, voices the same acute awareness of the reader and of sociocultural conditions as primary participants in the formation of novelistic aesthetics. By constructing a viable story through orthodox twentieth-century formal technique and subsequently proceeding to negate the validity of that viable story, Onetti brings to light the gullibility of the modern reader toward technique and formalistic methods.

In his agile use of the formal apparatus, the contemporary author has assumed a godlike countenance. As Vargas Llosa points out, the vacuum created by the death of God in western society is being filled by man's creative impulse, by his art, his novel, and formal aesthetics.[2] Eighteen years before the Peruvian novelist made these observations, Onetti was attempting to demythify the formal technique and the deified novelist through *Los adioses*. It should not surprise us, then, that this author, signaled by the same Vargas Llosa as the originator of Latin America's creative novel, should be also one of the first writers to warn us of the pitfalls of the creative process.

Similarly, *Para una tumba sin nombre* is an abnegation and systematic doubting of objective reality, whether it be the natural reality which constitutes the early twentieth-century Latin American novel, exemplified by Eustasio Rivera and Rómulo Gallegos, or the reality of the human circumstance which forms the socially committed indigenous novel. Onetti's intent with this short novel, which appeared four years after *Los adioses*, was by no means an overt attempt at negating what Vargas Llosa calls our "primitive novel." It was, rather, an effort to question the absolute meaning and value of "vulgar" reality which the artifice of aesthetics transforms into art, all art and art of all times. As such, Onetti's work transcends temporal and regional boundaries and ventures into the universal realm of creativity.

Reality in *Para una tumba* is rendered relative, fluid, and elastic. It acquires its meaning and qualities through a phenomenological process. The individual's perceptive mechanism, the artist's visual and moral angle, is what makes objective phenomena and events meaningful. These precepts concerning reality are, of course, not new in Onetti with this particular novel. The very same principles of reality's aesthetic and moral value formed the formal basis of all of Onetti's previous works. In this particular novel, however, the contrasting and juxtaposition of drastically differing viable stories based on the same set of objective and "actual" realities accentuate the emphasis of these principles. Insofar as Onetti is a creative rather than a primitive writer, to use Vargas Llosa's dichotomies, he is a "humanist" rather than a naturalistic-anthropomorphic writer in that he attempts to objectify something subjective, the reverse process of his predecessors. The emerging reality, therefore, emanates not from nature but from the subjective psyche of the individual, whether it be the author's, reader's, or character's. Clearly the resultant substance of objectifying, that is to say, the reality which emerges in a work of art, is irrevocably dependent upon the apparatus and *modus operandi* (the aesthetics) which the artist and reader bring to the process of creating.

In works like *Los adioses* and *Para una tumba sin nombre* we witness Onetti's emphatic and overt awareness of this creative process. For a writer like Onetti, aesthetics *is* the work and, conversely, a work of art is fundamentally its aesthetics. This is the significance of Vargas Llosa's affirmation that "the new Latin American novelist recognizes that his success or failure as a creator will be decided not by the themes he selects, nor by the emotions or obsessions he expresses, but rather by the formal elements—words and structure—that are adopted to develop those themes, emotions, or obsessions."[3]

Implicit in Vargas Llosa's statement is a reaffirmation of Onetti's stance on aesthetics as it emerges from the two short novels under discussion. Although our judgment of a good or bad writer has come to depend upon the "formal elements" an author chooses to implement, it is obvious that the writer must have some substantive content (theses, obsessions, emotions) which he attempts to express. To forget this is to put the cart before the horse; it would mean falling into the maze of formalistic games in which the primacy of art is relegated to its technical machinations and not to its transcendent meaning. For true art—of lasting and universal value—must transcend not only the crude reality which it tries to order and transform but also its own means and artifices.

These self-reflective affirmations on the art of the novel accompany certain aesthetic experimentations by Juan Carlos Onetti. As a novelist who was fully cognizant of his fiction's inner workings and had attained artistic maturity two decades ago, Onetti, if not an originator, is certainly abreast of the vanguard which ushers in the new Latin American novel and its "boom." The innovative aspect of his novel within the tradition of the Latin American novel lies in elevating form and technique to an equal plane with reality and vision. Conversely, his work represents a reevaluation of man's circumstance and human condition vis-à-vis the artistic methods hitherto utilized for its conveyance and aesthetic representation. Compared to the daring experiments of the newest Latin American novel, Onetti was obviously still on the ground, whereas Vargas Llosa, Cabrera Infante, Severo Sarduy, and Manuel Puig are in full flight of aesthetic experimentation with the novelistic genre.

We should keep in mind, however, that *El pozo*, a work which speaks to us more coherently through its technical form and language than through its schizoid, substantive content, appears one year after Rubén Romero's *La vida inútil de Pito Pérez* (*The Useless Life of Pito Pérez*) (1938) and only two years before Ciro Alegría's *El mundo es ancho y ajeno* (*Broad and Alien Is the World*) (1941), the latter work beating out Onetti's second and never published novel for an international literary prize. That is to say, that when the novelistic vogue of the day was still the type of work which one could describe as a curious hybrid of Latin America's colonial chronicles and essays of its independence period, Onetti was engaged in paving the way for *Tres tristes tigres* (*Three Trapped Tigers*) and *Boquitas pintadas* (*Heartbreake Tango*). For we should not forget that in that same year of 1941 when Ciro Alegría's novel appeared, Juan Carlos Onetti published what could be considered a progenitor and River Plate version of *Tres tristes tigres*. I am speaking, of course, of *Tierra de nadie*, that masquerade in a no-man's-land of a forsaken community of men and women, inextricably trapped by the petrified nonentity of their essence and its environment.

Tierra de nadie is a work whose content, vision, as well as its transcendent artistic value, are highly dependent upon language, technique, and style. A contextual focus clearly indicates the anachronistic character of Onetti and of his fiction. For *Tierra de nadie* is neither essay nor chronicle, but a conscious attempt to elevate narrative technique, language, and setting to a plane of vision and content, an attempt to equalize medium and form with message, much like the achievement of Guillermo Cabrera Infante twenty-six years later.

The inanity of the language of *El pozo* and the senseless psyche which utters it are of a sanguineous relationship to the inanities that make up recent novels like *La traición de Rita Hayworth* (*Betrayed by Rita Hayworth*) and *Boquitas pintadas*. Rodríguez-Monegal states with respect to these two novels that what is really important in them "is that *continuum* of spoken language which is at the same time the vehicle of the narrative and the narrative itself. . . . The alienated language is alienation itself."[4] This statement could appropriately be applied to *El pozo;* it does describe Onetti's first work quite accurately up to a point. The difference between Onetti and Puig in this respect is only one of degree. Onetti's experimental novelty is of a speculative nature, whereas Puig's experiment has found concretization and, as such, it no longer is an experiment but an actualized application of aesthetic principles which were speculatively employed by Onetti. If we may speak of the Latin American novelistic tradition as a phenomenon of collective evolution, Puig's aesthetics are a culmination of a project begun by Juan Carlos Onetti.

Although daring and audacious for their time, Onetti's experiments still manifest a strong inhibition. As such, the medium, the means, and the aesthetics whose significance he is attempting to bring to light can only reach an equal plane with the message and vision of the author at their most radical stretch. With *El pozo*, for example, Onetti's attempt at conveying the individual's existential absurdity and his alienation is broached through his choice of personage, setting, narrative point of view, and style of language. There is still, however, a necessity felt by the author to go beyond what this use of technique and aesthetics *show*. He therefore creates a situation which must overtly *tell*. That is to say, he imbues his "hero" with a goal, a final attempt at its attainment, and inevitable failure, all of which bear witness to his language, to the ambience (physical as well as spatiotemporal), and to his appearance. The totality of all this, in turn, is saturated with the alienation and the absurdity of the human condition.

We see Onetti at the initial stage of his career straddling what eventually will become of the novel at the hand of someone like Puig or Sarduy and the traditional novel of late nineteenth- and early twentieth-century Europe. These younger novelists take the human situations, which Onetti found necessary to re-create, for granted. Thus, they see no necessity whatever to subject their characters to trial and failure. Their point of departure is the point of failure, alienation, and absurdity. As such, they need not demonstrate, show, or even tell. They simply expose, a method of exposure which is the hyperbole of that unmitigated objectivity tried by Onetti in works like *Tierra de nadie* and *Para esta noche*. In Puig's work, therefore, we are abandoned into the vacuous flow of words of a woman or of a boy. There is an inherent assumption on the part of the novelist that these absurd creatures and their inane locution bear some blood relation to us, a supposition which makes the author's presence superfluous. The assumption is proving accurate, as the great success of these newer novels attests. The danger, the borderline of nihilism of art, however, is imminent.

Juan Carlos Onetti's doubt and forewarnings about unchecked trust in reality and in uncontrolled novelistic techniques ring loud, as do Henry James' skepticism and distrust in the capacity of reality to be art without the artist. The end result remains to be seen. One could say, however, that the possibility of an evolutionary jump in the genre of the novel is not entirely out of the question within the Latin American context. The goal of the development begun by Onetti is tempting though difficult to assess. I think one can safely entertain as an alternative to artistic nihilism (to the nonnovel novel which reigns in France) the fabulation, the myth; alternatives which, in the novel, find in Juan Carlos Onetti one of their earliest exponents.

The mythical dimension in the tradition of the Latin American novel has in some mysterious and incomprehensible way always been present. Its presence in the primitive and naturalistic novel may be due to the all-devouring vastness and seemingly infinite geotemporal setting which permeates the novelist's psyche and imagination. For myth is a cosmological phenomenon and is borne of a feeling of spatial infinity and timelessness. Until the generation of writers like Miguel Ángel Asturias, Alejo Carpentier, Jorge Luis Borges, and Juan Carlos Onetti, the element of myth had remained a coincidental phenomenon but which seems to have existed of an inherent necessity, much like our incomprehensible unconscious. With these writers this element comes to the fore through a sharp focus which they, each in his individual way, concentrate on its ever-present incidence. Writers like Asturias and Carpentier use myths which form an integral part of the American consciousness and spiritual psyche, as a lens through which the cosmos and vision comprising their work take on new significance and shades of meaning. We could trace more contemporary works of mythification like Lezama Lima's *Paradiso* and Carlos Fuentes' *La región más transparente (Where the Air Is Clear)* to the work of these writers.

On the other hand, there is another group of writers, to which Juan Carlos Onetti belongs, engaged in the fabulation of the peculiarly American human condition, rural as well as urban. This type of fabulation is myth born of man's experience, but it is as compelling as the mysterious and occult myth which forms an inherent part of the American psyche. One can say that this second group of writers mythologizes the daily existence rather than exposes the eminently unconscious. Leopoldo Marechal, first in this long line of novelists, epitomizes the elevation of the human experience to myth. His attempt, by no means unlike that of James Joyce's *Ulysses*, tries to give a totality and cosmic proportions to an

148   JUAN CARLOS ONETTI

actual human environment within the confines of the novel. His example is brought to perfection in a work like Cabrera Infante's *Tres
tristes tigres* (*Three Trapped Tigers*) or Vargas Llosa's *La casa verde*
(*The Green House*) which expands its boundaries from city to nation. João Güimarães Rosa's *Grande sertão veredas* (*The Devil to
Pay in the Backlands*) is Brazil's version of this kind of mythical
fabulation.

Juan Carlos Onetti, and more recently Gabriel García Márquez,
however, mythologize on the plane of allegory, that is to say,
through a cosmos of their own invention paralleling the realm of actual experience. The world of Santa María represents an aesthetic
rejuvenation in Onetti's fiction. The metempsychosis to myth
supplied the author with a viable alternative and new impetus at a
point of metaphysical and aesthetic impasse. With this alternative
Onetti overcame an ominous nihilism and fruitfully extended his
creative lifeline in 1950 with the appearance of *La vida breve*. This
development seems to be the dominant and by far the most powerful one in the contemporary Latin American novel.

Although this predominating new direction appears to have been
derived by common agreement by these novelists, in actuality the
more contemporary Latin American novelist is as individualistic and
as skeptical toward commonly derived and predetermined
aesthetics as Juan Carlos Onetti has been since the beginning of his
career. Any concurrence within the vision and aesthetics of the new
novel should therefore be attributed to the common American experience of these writers. The Latin American novel today, deriving
its homogeneity from very heterodox styles and approaches, points
toward the universal nature of man's condition regardless of the
means by which the art rendering it is derived. This, I suppose, is
another way of saying that the Latin American novelist today is
creating universal art. Juan Carlos Onetti's indispensable role in this
endeavor I hope has been justly documented in the foregoing
pages.

Notes and References

Preface

1. Jean Paul Sartre, *Literary Essays* (New York, 1957), p. 23.
2. Joseph Conrad, "Novel as World," in *The Theory of the Novel*, 2d ed., ed. Philip Stevick (New York, 1967), p. 29.

Chapter One

1. Geoffrey Hartman, "Structuralism: the Anglo-American Adventure," in *Structuralism*, ed. Jacques Ehrmann (New York, 1970), p. 150.
2. Philip Stevick, *The Theory of the Novel*, 2d ed. (New York, 1967), p. 185.
3. Richard M. Ohmann, "Prologomena to the Analysis of Prose Style," in *The Theory of the Novel*, p. 206.
4. Ibid., pp. 199 - 200.
5. Susan Langer, *Feeling and Form* (New York, 1953), p. 258.
6. Ohmann, p. 204
7. Ibid., p. 206
8. Juan Carlos Onetti, "El pozo," in *Obras Completas*, ed. Emir Rodríguez-Monegal (Mexico City, 1970), p. 49. All subsequent references to Onetti's works are from the *Obras Completas*, hereafter cited as *oc*.
9. María Esther Gilio. Interview with Onetti in *Marcha* (July 1, 1966):

Gilio: En cuanto a su propia relación con el mundo. . . .
Onetti: Usted dice que no estoy inmerso en él; que me niego a aceptarlo.
Gilio: Sí, y digo también que para construir su literatura no mira al exterior sino al mundo que tiene en sus entrañas. Se desentiende de la historia.
Onetti: El mundo que tengo en mis entrañas. . . . La frase es novedosa y tiene fuerza. Pero, ese mundo que yo tengo en mis entrañas, mi querida señora, es una consecuencia de lo que usted llama el mundo exterior. Un mundo en el que estoy inserto y que acepto. Me reservo el derecho de criticarlo y lo hago en el estilo indirecto y escéptico que usted me conoce.
Gilio: Su mundo literario también es distorsionado. Tanta distorsión no se le hace sospechosa? Verdaderamente usted cree que acepta el mundo exterior?
Onetti: Esto me hace recordar la definición de un famoso pintor francés: "El artista debe actuar frente a la realidad como actúa el amante frente a la mujer: la ama pero no la respeta." Hablamos de otra cosa?

10. Carlos Maggi, *Gardel, Onetti y algo más* (Montevideo, 1967), pp. 95 - 97:

149

Él está ahí; jadea. Se oye un sonido grave, amarillo y ancho como el pito de un barco dentro de la niebla; una ballena enferma—diría O'Neill—quejándose en el patio del fondo; un gran crustáceo desmantelado, un caballo abatido, de ojos lentos, intimidado; algo tierno derrumbado en el tragaluz de una sucia casa de apartamentos, naufragado bajo el polvo triste que llovizna sobre las ciudades. . . . Come su comida fría, fuma minuciosamente, bebe largo vino tinto sin buscar a nadie como llorando al revés, hacia dentro, por lo que se escapa y se pierde mientras el humo se disuelve entre las cuatro paredes de su pozo de aire. . . . Apasionadamente desapasionado, cree que no cree en nada y sólo tiene fe en la falta de fe. Hay muy pocas cosas que le importen (tal vez la pureza pura con garant)a de imposible) y sin embargo se desvela por todas las cosas. Detiene la noche y sobre un cuaderno escolar, compone, provoca la vida dentro de su vida.

11. Luis Harss and Barbara Dohman, *Into the Mainstream* (New York, 1967), pp. 173 - 74.

12. Cited by Leonard Lutwack, "Mixed and Uniform Prose Styles in the Novel," in *The Theory of the Novel*, p. 214.

13. Emir Rodríguez-Monegal, "Una o dos historias de amor, *Los adioses* de Juan Carlos Onetti," in his *Narradores de esta América* (Montevideo, 1961), pp. 173 - 82.

14. Lutwack, p. 217

15. Ibid., p. 218

Chapter Two

1. Virginia Woolf, "Mr. Bennett and Mrs. Brown," in *Approaches to the Novel*, ed. Robert Scholes (San Francisco, 1961), pp. 211 - 30.

2. Nathalie Sarraute, *The Age of Suspicion: Essays on the Novel*. Translated by Maria Jolas (New York, 1963).

3. E. M. Forster, *Aspects of the Novel* (New York, 1927), p. 63.

4. Jaime Concha, "Sobre *Tierra de nadie* de Juan Carlos Onetti," *Atenea* 417 (1967), 179: "El lector aprehende únicamente pasados y futuros actualizados."

5. Ibid., p. 175: "los personajes no reconocen sino el campo preciso de su experiencia subjetiva."

6. Caracé Hernández, "Juan Carlos Onetti: pistas para sus laberintos," *Mundo Nuevo* 34 (1967), 65 - 72: "instrumentos o personificaciones demiúrgicas, sin fulgor propio."

7. Mario Benedetti, "Juan Carlos Onetti y la aventura del hombre," in his *Literatura Uruguaya del siglo XX* (Montevideo, 1963), p. 76.

8. Harss and Dohmann, p. 174.

9. R. W. B. Lewis, "William Faulkner: The Hero in the New World," in *Faulkner*, ed. Robert Penn Warren (Englewood Cliffs, N.J., 1966), p. 206.

10. Jaime Concha, "El sueño compartido en *Tierra de nadie*," unpublished manuscript, 1966.

11. Ángel Rama, "Epilogue" to *El pozo*, 2d ed. (Montevideo, 1965),

p. 66: "es la soledad la que genera la imperiosa necesidad de escribir. Se es escritor . . . cuando se está en soledad absoluta."

12. Concha, "El sueño compartido . . ." "Con un análisis entre frío y patético, Llarvi ha podido precisar tres momentos en el proceso de la autoconciencia: el despojamiento de lo social, la conciencia de la propia carne y la experiencia de la nadidad engañosa del ser interior" (p. 20).

13. Rodríguez-Monegal, *Narradores de esta America* (Montevideo, 1961), pp. 155 - 73.

14. Rodríguez-Monegal, prologue to *Obras completas* of Onetti, p. 21.

15. Ibid., prologue, p. 24

16. Jean Paul Sartre, "John Dos Passos and *1919,*" in *Literary Essays* (New York, 1957), p. 91.

17. Jean Paul Sartre, *Being and Nothingness* (New York, 1956), pp. 608 - 11.

Chapter Three

1. See Leon Edel, *The Modern Psychological Novel* (New York, 1964).

2. Günter Blöcker, "William Faulkner," in *Faulkner,* p. 122.

3. Jean Pouillon, "Time and Destiny in Faulkner," *Faulkner,* p. 82.

4. Ibid., p. 84.

5. Victor Brombert, *The Intellectual Hero: Studies in the French Novel 1880 - 1955* (Chicago, 1960).

6. James Irby, *Influencia de Faulkner en cuatro narradores hispanoamericanos* (Mexico City, 1956), p. 90.

7. Concha, "El sueño compartido . . .": "Onetti reduce a Buenos Aires a débiles menciones fragmentarias, a esquinas de calles, a uno que a otro rascacielo, a un reflejo de letrero luminoso, a la presencia intermitente del río. . . . Despedazada en trozos dispersos, reducida a vestigios de situaciones humanas, la microtopografía bonaerense materializa la ruina espiritual de sus habitantes" (p. 3).

8. Irby, p. 79.

9. Concha, "Sobre *Tierra de nadie*" "Cada ser es una momia de su propio pasado" (p. 183).

10. Jean Paul Sartre, "On *The Sound and the Fury:* Time in the Work of Faulkner," in *Literary Essays*, p. 79.

11. Harss and Dohmann, p. 194.

12. I do not include here Ossorio of *Para esta noche* because of the melodramatic nature of his actions.

13. Lawrence S. Kubie, "William Faulkner's *Sanctuary,*" in *Faulkner,* p. 144.

14. Karsten Harries, *The Meaning of Modern Art: A Philosophical Interpretation* (Evanston, Ill., 1968), p. 110; my italics.

Chapter Four

1. See Wayne C. Booth, "Distance and Point of View: An essay in Classification," *Essays in Criticism* 11 (1961), 60 - 71.

2. *The Modern Psychological Novel* (New York, 1964).

3. Percy Lubbock, *The Craft of Fiction* (New York, 1969), p. 62.

4. Jean Paul Sartre, "François Mauriac and Freedom," in *Literary Essays*, p. 7.

5. Ibid., p. 23

6. Mario Vargas Llosa, "Primitives and Creators," *Times Literary Supplement*, November 14, 1968, pp. 1287 - 88.

7. Edel, p. 198.

8. Rodríguez-Monegal, prologue, p. 29.

9. Harries, p. 52

10. Norman Friedman, "Point of View in Fiction: The Development of a Critical Concept," *Publication of the Modern Language Association of America* 70 (1955).

11. Harss and Dohmann, p. 185

12. Rodríguez-Monegal, prologue, p. 28.

13. Rodríguez-Monegal, *Narradores* . . . , p. 178.

14. Jorge Luis Borges, "Pascal's Sphere," in *Other Inquisitions 1937 - 1952* (Austin, 1964), p. 9

15. Rodríguez-Monegal, *Narradores* . . . , p. 180.

Chapter Five

1. R. S. Crane, "The Concept of Plot and the Plot of *Tom Jones*," in *Critics and Criticism: Ancient and Modern* (Chicago, 1952), pp. 616 - 48.

2. Norman Friedman, "Forms of the Plot," in *The Theory of the Novel*, p. 150.

3. Jorge Luis Borges citing Carlyle, "Partial Enchantments of the *Quixote*," in *Other Inquisitions 1937 - 1952*, p. 46.

4. I equate the two terms on the basis offered by René Wellek and Austin Warren, *Theory of Literature* (New York, 1942), p. 216.

5. Jorge Luis Borges, "Nathaniel Hawthorne," in *Other Inquisitions*, p. 63.

6. Ibid., "Time and J. W. Dunne," in *Other Inquisitions*, p. 21.

7. Ángel Rama, epilogue to *El pozo*, 2d ed. (Montevideo, 1965).

8. Victor Brombert, *The Intellectual Hero: Studies in the French Novel 1880 - 1955* (Chicago, 1960).

9. Concha, "El sueño compartido en *Tierra de nadie*" "Su ley radica en que la serie se constituye sobre un desajuste entre lo anunciado y realizado; pero esta infidelidad y proyecto esbozado, en sí misma expresiva de una voluntad inestable, está metódicamente regulada" (p. 17).

10. Ibid., p. 17

11. Brombert, *The Intellectual Hero*, p. 188.

12. Rodríguez-Monegal, prologue, p. 21.

13. Ibid., p. 22.

14. Ibid., p. 40.

15. Ibid., p. 31.

Chapter Six

1. Juan Carlos Onetti, *Tiempo de abrazar* (Montevideo, 1974), p. 146; hereafter cited as *T*.

2. Jorge Ruffinelli rightfully points out in his introduction to *Tiempo de abrazar* that this fragment contains the germinal nucleus of the mythical Santa María, its Dr. Díaz Grey (and Elena Sala) who will become explicitly conceived as integral parts of the Onettian cosmogony with *La vida breve*. The reference in "Excursión" reads: "This new doctor is very good, he cares a great deal. . . . Elena was telling me when he enters the room [sala] . . ." ("Este médico de ahora es muy bueno, se preocupa mucho. . . . Me decía Elena cuando entra en la sala . . .). The sketchy description of the provincial country town, Ruffinelli claims, may be a prototype of the mythical Santa María.

Chapter Seven

1. For a succinct discussion of this aspect of the new novel see Mario Vargas Llosa, "The Latin American Novel Today," *Books Abroad* 44 (1970), 7 - 16; and Emir Rodríguez-Monegal, "The New Latin American Novel," same issue of *Books Abroad*, pp. 45 - 50.

2. Vargas Llosa, "The Latin American Novel Today," p. 12.

3. Ibid., p. 10.

4. Rodríguez-Monegal, "The New Latin American Novel," p. 49.

Selected Bibliography

1. Novels

El pozo. Montevideo: Ediciones Signo, 1939.
Tierra de nadie. Buenos Aires: Editorial Losada, 1941.
Para esta noche. Buenos Aires: Poseidón, 1943.
La vida breve. Buenos Aires: Editorial Sudamericana, 1950.
Los adioses. Buenos Aires: Editorial Sur, 1954.
Para una tumba sin nombre. Montevideo: Marcha, 1959.
La cara de la desgracia. Montevideo: Alfa, 1960.
El astillero. Buenos Aires: Compañía General Fabril Editora, 1961.
Tan triste como ella. Montevideo: Alfa, 1963.
Juntacadáveres. Montevideo: Alfa, 1964.
La muerte y la niña. Buenos Aires: Corregidor, 1973.
Tiempo de abrazar. Montevideo: Arca, 1974. Includes an introductory essay by Jorge Ruffinelli, short stories written between 1933 and 1950 some of which have never been collected into editions of the author's works previously. A fragment hitherto unedited of what was to have been a novel "Los niños en el bosque" is also included.

2. Collections of Short Stories and Novels

Un sueño realizado y otros cuentos. Montevideo: Número, 1951.
El infierno tan temido. Montevideo: Asir, 1962.
Jacob y el otro. Un sueño realizado y otros cuentos. Montevideo: Ediciones de la Banda Oriental, 1965.
Tres Novelas. Montevideo: Alfa, 1967.
Cuentos completos. Buenos Aires: CEDAL, 1967.
La novia robada y otros cuentos. Buenos Aires: CEDAL, 1968.
Los rostros del amor. Edited by Emir Rodríguez-Monegal. Buenos Aires: CEDAL, 1968. An anthology.
Cuentos cortos completos. Caracas: Monte Avila Editores, 1968.
Novelas cortas completas. Caracas: Monte Avila Editores, 1968.
Obras completas. Edited by Emir Rodríguez-Monegal. México: Aguilar, 1970.

3. Collected Articles and Essays

Requiem por Faulkner y otros escritos. Montevideo: Arca, 1976.

4. English Translations

a. Novels

The Shipyard (El astillero). Translated by Rachel Caffyn. New York: Scribner's, 1968.

155

A Brief Life (La vida breve). Translated by Hortense Carpentier. New York: Grossman, 1976.

b. Short stories:

"Jacob and the Other." In *Prize Stories from Latin America: Winners of the Life en españOL Literary Contest*. Translated by Izaak A. Langnas. New york: Doubleday, 1963.

"Welcome, Bob." Translated by Hanna Edwards. *Odyssey Review* 3, no. 2 (1963), 192 - 99.

"Dreaded Hell." In *Latin American Writing Today*, edited by J. M. Cohen, pp. 34 - 48. Baltimore: Penguin, 1967.

"A Dream Come True." In *Doors and Mirrors: Fiction and Poetry from Spanish America*, edited by Hortense Carpentier and Janet Brof, pp. 190 - 203. New York: Grossman Publishers, 1972.

SECONDARY SOURCES

1. Books and Articles

DEREDITA, JOHN. "The Shorter Works of Juan Carlos Onetti." *Studies in Short Fiction* 8, no. 1 (1971), 112 - 22. An excellent, succinct introduction to Onetti's shorter prose. Professor Deredita's study is a most appropriate complement to my volume which deals, for the most part, with the author's more extensive prose.

HARSS, LUIS, and DOHMANN, BARBARA. "Juan Carlos Onetti or the Shadows on the Wall." In *Into the Mainstream*. New York: Harper and Row, 1967. A good introduction to Onetti for the student and general reader. In this interview the authors attempt to capture the quality of Onetti's surroundings, moods, and general tone of his attitudes as reflected in his work.

IRBY, JAMES E. *La influencia de William Faulkner en cuatro narradores hispanoamericanos*. Mexico City: Universidad Autónoma de México, 1956. A master's thesis in which Professor Irby deals with earlier works of Onetti. While his observations are germane and very valuable, Onetti's most important works have appeared since this study.

RODRIGUEZ-MONEGAL, EMIR. Prologue to *Obras Completas* by Juan Carlos Onetti. México City: Aguilar, 1970. An excellent overall introduction to Onetti by the most well-versed critic and scholar of the author's work. The prologue consists of ten sections, each focusing on specific aspects of Onetti's development and the evolution of his work. For the most part the information is culled from the numerous essays Rodríguez-Monegal has written. The synthesis is a most informative statement.

RUFINELLI, JORGE. "Onetti antes de Onetti." Introduction to *Tiempo de abrazar* by Juan Carlos Onetti. Montevideo: Arca, 1974. Focuses on the early years. Ruffinelli discusses the author's first stories and

fragments and their relationship to later, better known works. The
study fills a previous lacuna in Onetti scholarship.

VERANI, HUGO. "Los comienzos: tres cuentos de Onetti anteriores a *El
pozo.*" *Hispamérica* 2 (1972), 27 - 34. Before Verani's article it was
commonly believed that *El pozo* was Onetti's first work. "Avenida de
Mayo—Diagonal—Avenida de Mayo," "El obstáculo," and "El posible Baldi," Onetti's first short stories dating from the early 1930s are
discussed.

2. Collected Studies

a. English

KADIR, DJELAL, ed. "Focus on Juan Carlos Onetti's *A Brief Life.*" *Review*
75 (Winter, 1975), 4 - 33. A special section of this issue coincides with
the publication of *La vida breve* in English translation. The "Focus"
includes, in addition to my foreword and chronology of Onetti, essays
by Professors Emir Rodríguez-Monegal, Hugo Verani, John
Deredita, Zunilda Gertel, and George Levine. It also includes a
poem, "La vida breve" by the Mexican writer José Emilio Pacheco.
Those interested in Onetti's *oeuvre* will find the essays on this key
work extremely suggestive.

b. Spanish

GRANDE, FELIX, ed. *Cuadernos Hispanoamericanos* 292 - 294 (October -
December, 1974), 7 - 750. This triple issue of the *Cuadernos* is the
most extensive single volume dedicated to Onetti. It includes a poem
by the author, as well as various other texts; a series of poems
dedicated to Onetti; a section of photographs of Onetti and his surroundings; critical essays on his work; a very extensive bibliography
of primary and secondary sources compiled by Professor Hugo
Verani. The volume is strongly recommended.

Index

(All works listed by authors' names. Titles mentioned in the text listed by English title first if the works have been translated.)